feel GOOD *with* FOOD

Asparagus

*Spiced Sprouting
Bean Salad*

feel GOOD *with* FOOD

Kumud Shah

To my children Lavina and Kunal for appreciating good food.

To my loving grandchildren Sai, Saj and Sahil

Welcome to the world of good food.

Sai, Sahil and Saj

Kunal and Jeni's vegetarian dog Lola

Feel Good with Food by Kumud Shah
First Published in Great Britain in 2009
Second Publication 2010
Published by Kumud Shah
Copyright 2009 Kumud Shah
www.kumudshah.com
A catalogue record for this book is available from the British Library.

ISBN: 978-0-9562885-0-9
Editor: Jenifer Courtney
Co-designed & styled: Lavina Mehta & Shaila Shah
Design: Sanath Nanayakkara, Kolourbox UK
Art Direction: Lavina Mehta
Typesetting: Lavina Mehta
Photography: Dilip Shelat
Photography styling by: Lavina Mehta
Make-up Artist: Genevieve Dean
Printer: Imprint Digital
Website: Kunal Shah

Neither the author nor the publishers can be held responsible for any claims arising from the irresponsible use of any dietary regime. Always consult your doctor with your existing health problems. This book is mainly a recipe book, the advice it contains is just a guideline for general wellbeing.

The information in this book is correct at the time of publication.

Contents

Acknowledgements   6

Introduction   7

Chapters

1 Cruciferous Vegetables   13

2 Leafy Greens   25

3 Tomatoes   41

4 Soya Beans   55

5 Red, Orange, Yellow and Green Vegetables   65

6 Rainbow Coloured Fruits   87

7 Beans, Peas and Lentils   97

8 Grains   111

9 Nuts and Seeds   123

Glossary   136
        Rainbow fruits and vegetables
        Vitamins
        Pre-biotic and pro-biotic
        Spices
        Cholesterol, fats and oils

Recipe Suggestions   142

Bibliography   144

*One cannot think well
love well, sleep well,
if one has not dined well*

Virginia Woolf

Acknowledgements

It is a thrill to teach cooking, a subject which I love very much. Writing this book has been a pure joy, a journey through teaching, tasting, trying and cooking delicious food. I feel I cannot be luckier than this!

Acknowledgements go to some very special people who have inspired and encouraged me to write this book.

Many, many thanks to my loving daughter, Lavina, for being with me through every page of this book, during and after her pregnancy. Your strong and dedicated commitment in trying to finish this book while nursing my grandson Sahil is most appreciated. Without your hard work of typing and re-writing, this book would not have taken shape. My loving son, Kunal and his partner Jeni for editing all the recipes and tasting and appreciating mum's food. Sacrificing your valuable time to help me is very heartwarming and endearing. Thank you for all your enthusiasm and encouragement, which gave me the strength to go forward.

Lavina's husband, Menal, and my husband, Kishore, for the support, love and all the background work in getting this book on the shelf. I am truly thankful for all the time you spent on the phone with the printer and the photographer, to make this a colourful book.

My gratitude to my younger sister Shaila, who fortunately happened to travel to London just in time before we sent the book to the designer. Shaila lovingly helped with the design of the stunning cover and the formatting of the text.

Thanks to Dilip Shelat, our photographer, for his creative ideas and beautiful pictures which have brought my 'food to life' in this book.

I am truly grateful to Moira Duncan, who proof read the book – what a godsend! Not only is she a student of mine but she's also a neighbour. Your help and resourceful suggestions are most appreciated.

A great pillar of strength has been Ramesh Kansagra and his family. I am thankful for your moral support, and warm well wishes.

A special thanks to Waitrose for supplying the fresh fruit and vegetables for all the photographs, and to John Lewis for letting me use many of the beautiful props.

Finally, this book is also dedicated to all my students who have attended my cookery classes – your positive feedback convinced me that all these recipes "work wonders"!

I hope this book is a stepping stone for your healthy future. I also hope you all cook these recipes, make positive changes to your eating patterns and take a step forward to a healthier lifestyle full of energy and vitality.

What better gift, than this "gift of health", could you offer someone you love and care for?

All the information written in this book is from research papers and books I have read over the years. It is just a guideline to encourage everyone to eat more plant-based foods, fruits and whole grains. A lot more research and scientific trials need to be done to prove all the data, but that might be too late for some of us, so it is in our best interests to act now. It is exciting to cook the recipes I have suggested, enjoy the food and hopefully delay the onset of illness so often associated with ageing.

"Happy cooking – Happy eating!"

Introduction

This book is about enjoying cooking and eating life's natural health-boosting plant-based foods. Research studies have shown that a high dietary intake of fruits and vegetables as well as whole grains is strongly associated with a reduced risk of developing chronic diseases such as cancer and cardiovascular disease (CVD), which are the top two causes of death in most industrialised countries. The government's "Five a Day" programme was developed as a guideline to increase public awareness of the health benefits of fruits, vegetables and the consumption of whole grains.

We are spoilt for choice of food varieties in this country, with fresh fruits, vegetables, grains, beans and nuts available to us throughout the year. We have every opportunity to eat well, so when we go shopping, faced with so much choice, what should we buy? To live longer, look younger and stay in good health what should we eat?

Thousands of biologically active phytochemicals (from the Greek word "phyto" meaning plant chemicals) have been identified in plant-based foods. These compounds protect the plant from harmful radiation, microbes and other damaging effects, and hopefully by eating plant-based foods we can benefit from the protection provided by the phytochemicals.

PHYTOCHEMICALS:

These are defined as, bioactive, both essential and non-essential nutrients from plant compounds. Non-essential phytochemicals can be classified as carotenoids, phenolics, alkaloids, nitrogen containing compounds and organosulfur compounds. *(Ref paper: Rui Hai Liu, 2004).*

The most studied non-essential dietary phytochemicals are carotenoids and phenolics.

Carotenoids:

More than 600 different carotenoids have been identified. Widely researched are alpha carotene, beta carotene, cyrptoxanthin, lutein, zeaxanthin, astaxanthin and lycopene. Carotenoids act as antioxidants.

Phenolics:

These are also powerful antioxidants and are subdivided into flavonoids, phenolic acid, stilbenes, coumarins and tannins. (Flavonoids and phenolic acids provide the most phenolics in our food).

Flavonoids:

More than 4,000 individual flavonoids have been identified. Flavonoids provide two thirds of phenolics in our diet. Flavonoids are potent antioxidants, but their effect has not been fully studied in humans.

Phenolic acids:

Provide one third of phenolics in our diet. They are components of cellulose, lignins, organic acids (for example, ferulic acids present in wheat bran; cholorogenic acids' oxidation leads to browning in apples and potatoes).

Supporting data from epidemiological studies, in-vitro, animal and clinical studies suggest the phytochemicals act as:

Antioxidants
Blood thinning agents
Blood sugar regulators
Anti-inflammatory, antibacterial, antiviral agents
Toxin neutralisers
Anti-carcinogens
Immune system stimulators
(Ref: Lampe J.W. Page)

A group of phytochemicals that have received a lot of attention and research for their health benefits are the **Antioxidants** which include:
Non-essential phytochemical antioxidants:
Phenolics
Carotenoids

Essential phytochemical antioxidants:
Vitamin C
Vitamin E
Minerals like selenium and manganese etc.

Research suggests that the antioxidants protect the body from free radical damage. Free radicals, molecules that carry one or more unpaired electrons, are largely formed as a result of the energy producing normal processes of cells. Oxygen is needed to carry out basic metabolic functions in the body and often this leads to the formation of pro-oxidants or super oxides – unstable oxygen molecules called free radicals.

Free radical production can be increased by environmental pollution, tobacco smoke, UV radiation and infection.

These unstable free radicals generally attack the nearest stable molecule, stealing its electron to gain stability, thus creating another free radical. **The antioxidant defence system interrupts the free radical chain reaction of oxidation, or scavenge and disable free radicals before they react with the body's cellular components.**

Oxidation by free radicals can alter the structure and function of several cellular components such as lipid containing cell membrane, proteins, RNA and DNA in the cells (which can mutate and become cancerous).

Antioxidants from the diet and from the body's internal antioxidant systems, work to quench or neutralise excess free radicals. However, over production of free radicals can cause an imbalance, leading to **oxidative stress.** This oxidative stress is linked in the development of chronic diseases like cancer, cardiovascular diseases, type 2 diabetes, Alzheimer's disease, inflammatory disorders and the ageing process – these are some of the most serious health problems in the Western world.

Give your body a helping hand to avoid oxidative stress by eating extra dietary antioxidants found in fruits, vegetables and whole grains. An everyday example to understand oxidation is to remember when an apple is cut in half, it starts to turn brown and to slow this oxidative damage, one rubs it with lemon juice, not knowing that lemon juice has the antioxidant vitamin C.

Isn't it frightening to realise that a similar oxidative damage could be happening in our body! The best reasons for eating fruits, vegetables, whole grains and other plant foods containing a wide variety of phytochemicals with extra antioxidants is to slow or delay this "rusting" of or oxidative damage to our vital organs. At the same time, some free radicals are essential to our survival to destroy harmful micro organisms; free radicals are crucial in producing hormones and activating certain enzymes.

To prevent or slow the oxidative stress induced by free radicals, sufficient amounts of dietary antioxidants need to be consumed.

I have selected the main and most researched to date categories of phytonutrients from plant-based foods, like carotenoids, phenolics, organosulfur compounds, fibres, EFA Omega 3 and Omega 6, antioxidants vitamin E and vitamin C, found in our daily diet, and created a broad spectrum of appetising recipes. **By cooking the recipes I suggest, unknowingly, you will benefit from their immune boosting phytonutrients and hopefully protect the body against illness.**

Food, especially fruits, contain natural **salicylates**, the chemical that aspirin is made of. The salicylates have anticoagulant,

anti-inflammatory and analgesic effects. Latest research on aspirin suggests that regular low doses help prevent heart attacks, strokes and colon cancer. Maybe low doses of salicylates from food have the same preventative effect as aspirin. It makes sense to eat fruits and vegetables and obtain natural salicylates. The foods which are extremely high in salicylates are blueberries, cherries, raspberries, spices used in Indian cooking and dried fruits like dates, currants and prunes.

Anticancer agents were found to be more effective when several foods in a whole diet were combined. It's the range and variety of phytochemicals that count; these compounds work **"synergistically"**. No single antioxidant supplement can replace the combination of natural phytochemicals in fruits and vegetables in achieving the health benefits. We do not have a RDA for phytochemicals, higher doses of supplements can be toxic. Therefore it is not wise to take mega doses of purified phytochemicals as supplements before strong scientific evidence supports doing so.

It could also be that fruits and vegetables contain compounds which encourage the body's natural protection enzyme to fight chronic illnesses. Until the future, when more research has been done and we have a better understanding of how phytochemicals react in the body, it's better to cook the mouth watering recipes I have suggested, enjoy your food and unknowingly help your body to boost its immune system. Pills or tablets simply cannot mimic the balanced and natural combination of phytochemicals found in plant-based foods.

Most of the serious chronic diseases take a long time to develop in healthy people before one feels ill, so it is necessary to eat foods rich in phytochemicals daily, on a regular basis, which may help to protect against the development of degenerative diseases.

The current enthusiasm for healthy eating spread by regular articles in newspapers and magazines on the latest research work on phytochemicals has suddenly sparked everyone's awareness of gaining the maximum benefit from the food one eats. In fact exchanging tips on food and health is a favourite topic of discussion among everyone I know, **it is the new love for living a healthy lifestyle.**

There is a lot of evidence, some published and some yet to be published that confirms that certain foods contain more health promoting nutrients than others. Studies have shown that at least 1:3 people will develop cancer in their lifetime. Eating a minimum of 5 portions of fruits and vegetables each day alone could decrease the risk of cancer. This recommendation will soon increase to between 5 and 10 servings of a wide variety of fruits and vegetables every day.

Some countries already advise this recommendation to reduce the risk of chronic diseases and to meet the nutrient requirement

for optimum health. This may sound a lot but cooking and eating a vegetarian diet, consuming a lot of fruit and vegetables is easy. This is my main reason for writing an exciting, thought provoking and easy to follow recipe book. By cooking the recipes I recommend, you can easily maximise the family's intake of fruit and vegetables and enjoy the flavour bursting meals as well.

My book is more about delaying or preventing the onset of illness, and enjoying the cooking and eating of delicious food – sharing it with your family and friends – having a great quality of life until we reach the point of "no-return". Nobody knows what's round the corner but it is in our hands to take a positive step towards eating well, controlling what we put in our mouths: a helping hand towards our own destiny.

How good it feels when one can protect the "body machine", nurture it, feed it well and hope it keeps one in optimum health.

At a young age, when I studied Biological Sciences at the University of East Anglia, my specialism being genetics and microbiology, I had no idea that studying the "science of the body" would lead me to the "science of food". I always joke with my students at the cookery classes that I regularly give, that "I can talk on food, shop for food, cook and eat good food for 24 hours if need be!"

Being a vegetarian gives me an extra incentive to write a book like this which includes my every day food - fruits, vegetables, lentils, whole grains and fats from nuts and good oils. **(There are no egg or fish recipes in my book).** Also being born in an Indian family, spices have always played a prominent role in my cooking. It has been known since ancient times that spices and their essential oils contain a high concentration of phytochemicals to prevent and delay some of the most chronic diseases. For example, spices like ginger, cloves, all spice, cinnamon, turmeric etc. have one of the highest antioxidant concentrations of all food groups.

Our children's health is one of the top priorities for most of us. By cooking and feeding children tasty and nutritionally balanced meals, they will get into the habit of eating sensibly from an early age and with luck, hopefully avoid or delay illness later in life.

I have divided the book into chapters, according to the important phytonutrients in each chapter, each with its own introduction and relevant recipes, the chapters all overlap but each group has its own specific powerful, nutritional profile. Dividing the foods into different groups also makes it easy to go shopping for food. It will clearly answer my first question of what do we buy when we go shopping faced with so much choice? Remember to buy something from the main groups, for example, some *Cruciferous Vegetables* like broccoli, *Leafy Greens* like spinach, *Coloured Vegetables* like mixed peppers, some *Tomatoes,* some *Soya* products, some *Grains,* some *Lentils, Nuts,* good oil and a basket full of all the rainbow Coloured Fruits.

The research work on phytochemicals is a constantly evolving area, the future lies with the scientists and I hope they aim to do more clinical investigation and bring molecular biology and molecular genetics into nutrient research work. Also certain foods are more researched than others so we know the benefits of these foods. **In the future many unknown foods will become popular for their health benefits.**

If I could inspire you and convince you to start cooking the exciting recipes, eat healthily, make a difference to your lifestyle, make you feel energetic, happy and bring a smile to your face, this radiance can be reflected not only on you but also on your family and friends; then my purpose for this book will be complete.

The blessings come from above and if I can also smile knowing that I have touched someone, managed to make a little difference and achieved a big life changing step in someone's life, then this is the best gift I could ask for.

Some 2,500 years ago, the famous quotation of Hippocrates, the "father of modern medicine", is still the most convincing reason for writing this book:

"LET YOUR FOOD BE YOUR MEDICINE LET YOUR MEDICINE BE YOUR FOOD"

Chapter 1

Introduction   14

Broccoli and Potato Curry   15

Cabbage and Celeriac Curry   16

Cauliflower and Cashew Nut Curry   17

Cabbage and Couscous Parcels
with Carrot Sauce   19

Indian Pancakes with Cabbage, Carrot
and Mango Relish   20

Cabbage, Carrot and Mango Relish   21

Red Cabbage Coleslaw   22

Stir Fry Chinese Cabbage and Kohlrabi
with Walnut Dressing   23

Cruciferous Vegetables

Broccoli

Introduction

Cruciferous vegetables such as broccoli, cauliflower, cabbage, kale, pak choi, turnips, collard greens, mustard greens, radish, rocket leaves and watercress are all rich in phytochemicals. The name "cruciferous" relates to the cross shaped flowers of these vegetables. The characteristic pungence of vegetables like broccoli and cabbage is due to the sulphur compounds that protect both the plants and the people who eat them.

Cruciferous vegetables contain the phytochemicals, sulforaphane and indoles - research suggests that these compounds may stimulate production of anticancer enzymes and help to keep cancer at bay. In fact indoles may help to prevent breast cancer by blocking the action of the extra hormone oestrogen that can trigger the growth of tumours. Indole compounds in cruciferous vegetables are easily lost in cooking water, so use this cooking water as a stock; in fact it is better to either steam these vegetables, or eat them raw. All cruciferous vegetables are key sources of antioxidant carotenoids, antioxidant vitamin C, calcium and fibre.

People who have thyroid problems should eat cruciferous vegetables in moderation because they contain a compound called goitrogens, which can interfere with the function of the thyroid gland.

This particular selection of recipes will offer the opportunity to experiment with new dishes using these often overlooked nutritious vegetables. Spices particularly complement these vegetables as they minimise the strong flavour, lift the dishes and create a mouth watering flavour. Herbs and spices contain enormous quantities of disease-preventing phytochemicals which neutralise different kinds of free radicals. Therefore I have recipes for broccoli curry, cauliflower curry, cabbage curry and cabbage relish to accompany spicy pancakes. Also included are tasty side dishes of red cabbage and a Chinese cabbage salad.

The recipes in "Cruciferous" and the "Leafy Greens" can be used together, as they have similar phyto-nutrients. The reason for giving "Leafy Greens" a separate section is to emphasise the importance of spinach, kale and green vegetables.

I hope you can include cruciferous vegetables in your diet at least 3 or 4 times a week, or more, to stay in optimum health!

Savoy Cabbage

Broccoli and Potato Curry

This curry is similar to *"Aloo Gobi"* a popular Indian curry, which uses potato and cauliflower. However, my version uses broccoli which gives the dish more nutritional value while retaining the great taste.

The nutrient dense broccoli is a star food. Its folate content (vitamin B) helps maintain cardio vascular health, boosts the immune system and indole compounds, specially indole-3-carbinol, in broccoli all help to fight against cancers, especially breast cancer. Broccoli is a good source of the antioxidant carotenoids, lutein and zeaxanthin, it is also rich in antioxidant vitamin C, potassium and co-enzyme Co Q10.

Broccoli is available all year round at a very reasonable price so there is no excuse for not eating it! Try to get children into the habit of eating it regularly.

Serves 4

225g potatoes	1 teaspoon salt or less
1 small broccoli	½ teaspoon chilli powder
2 - 3 tablespoons oil	1 teaspoon garam masala
1 teaspoon cumin seeds	1 tablespoon dhana jeera
1 red onion - chopped	¼ teaspoon turmeric
6 cherry tomatoes - cut in half	1 teaspoon lime juice
3 - 4 spring onions - finely sliced	1 - 2 tablespoons natural yogurt

- Boil or steam the potatoes, peel and cut each one into 4 chunky pieces (if using new potatoes do not peel and keep them whole). Cut the broccoli into big florets, wash and parboil or steam for a few minutes, until tender.

- Warm the oil in a big pan, add the cumin seeds and the chopped onion. Stir for 4-5 minutes until the onion is soft. Add the tomatoes, salt, chilli powder, garam masala, dhana jeera, turmeric, lime juice and half a glass of water - let it cook for 3 minutes.

- Mix in the potatoes and broccoli and simmer on a low heat, covered, for about 10 minutes.

- For a thicker sauce, add the yogurt. Garnish with the sliced spring onions and serve.

Cabbage and Celeriac Curry

White cabbage, finely shredded and spiced is a favourite quick curry in most Indian households. My addition of an equal amount of grated celeriac turns this simple traditional dish into a very nutritious curry.

Celeriac is a root vegetable which provides fibre and vitamin B2. This may help to boost the immune system, regulate hormones and also relieve stress.

Cabbage juice helps to detoxify the liver and is an effective remedy for stomach ulcers.

Serves 2

2 handfuls cabbage - finely shredded	¼ teaspoon turmeric
2 handfuls celeriac - finely shredded	1 tablespoon dhana jeera
1 tablespoon oil	6 cherry tomatoes - halved
1 teaspoon cumin seeds	lime to taste
½ teaspoon salt	coriander leaves for garnish
½ teaspoon red chilli powder	

- Shred the cabbage. Peel the celeriac and shred it finely.

- Warm the oil in a saucepan, add the cumin seeds, cabbage and celeriac. Stir fry for 2-3 minutes. Add half a glass of water and cook for 5 minutes. Add all the spices - salt, chilli powder, turmeric and dhana jeera – mix well. Put a lid on the saucepan and cook for 10 minutes on medium heat.

- Stir in the cherry tomatoes. Add lime juice to taste and garnish with coriander leaves. Serve it hot as part of an Indian meal or cold with green mixed salad for a light lunch.

Celeriac

Cauliflower and Cashew Nut Curry

This dry curry can be served to accompany an Indian meal but I prefer to eat it cold with a green salad of baby spinach, watercress and rocket leaves.

Serves 2 - 4

8 florets of cauliflower
25 pieces of cashew nuts
1 tablespoon oil
½ teaspoon cumin seeds
½ teaspoon asafoetida

1 teaspoon salt or less
½ teaspoon red chilli powder
¼ teaspoon turmeric
1 tablespoon dhana jeera
lime to taste

- Blanch the cauliflower florets in boiling water for 4 minutes, then strain and cool. Alternatively steam the florets, until they are tender.

- Split the cashew nuts in two and soak in warm water for 15 minutes. Strain the cashew nuts.

- Warm the oil in a wok. Add the cumin seeds, asafoetida, cauliflower and cashew nuts.

- Stir fry for 3 minutes. Lower the heat and add the spices, salt, chilli powder, turmeric and dhana jeera. Cover the wok and cook for 5 minutes on a low heat – stir frequently.

- Add lime juice to taste.

Cashew Nuts

Cabbage and Couscous Parcels with Carrot Sauce

This Middle Eastern dish in vibrant green cabbage leaves looks and tastes exotic. The steamed parcels make a filling lunch dish, or can be served as individual portions as a starter before a main course.

Makes 4 parcels

4 big cabbage leaves – use Savoy cabbage

For the cabbage filling:

100g couscous - 4 heaped tablespoons

200ml hot stock

2 tablespoons olive oil

½ red onion - finely chopped

½ red pepper - de-seeded and diced

½ courgette - small cubes

3-4 florets broccoli - finely chopped

1 tablespoon pine nuts or pumpkin seeds

5 dry apricots or any dry fruits - chopped

salt to taste

2 tablespoon flat leaf parsley - chopped

lime juice to taste

For the carrot sauce:

1 tablespoon olive oil

3 medium sized carrots - chopped

½ red onion

½ red pepper

1 small potato - sweet potato if available

450 ml hot stock or water

½ teaspoon salt

- Parboil each cabbage leaf for 1 minute in hot water to preserve the green colour, drain each leaf and let it cool. Use this water as stock for the carrot sauce.

- Add 2 teaspoons of good quality stock powder to 200ml hot water. Add this hot stock to the couscous and let it soak for 10 minutes. (Alternatively use home made vegetable stock)

- In a big saucepan, add 2 tablespoons of oil and sauté the onion, red pepper, courgette, broccoli, pine nuts/pumpkin seeds and apricots for 5 minutes. Switch off the pan. Add the couscous and parsley and season well.

- Cut the thick stem out of each cabbage leaf. Fill each leaf with 2 tablespoons of the above mixture to form a parcel and arrange on a steamer tray. Steam for 10 minutes until the cabbage parcels are just cooked.

- For the carrot sauce, heat the oil in a saucepan and sauté the chopped carrots, red onion, red pepper and potato for 5 minutes. Add the stock or water and cook for 25 minutes. Using a hand blender, blend it well to a thick sauce consistency and season with salt. Serve this hot sauce with the cabbage parcels.

Cabbage and Couscous Parcels.
Apple and cranberry spritzer

Indian Pancakes with Cabbage, Carrot and Mango Relish

These Gujarati pancakes made from gram (chickpea) flour and known as pudlas, are a popular, light, savoury lunch dish. Serve them with yogurt or cabbage, carrot and mango relish.

Makes 6 pancakes

225g gram flour	I teaspoon salt
I teaspoon chilli powder	¼ teaspoon turmeric
I teaspoon cumin seeds - dry-roasted	2 tablespoons fresh coriander - chopped
I teaspoon ajwain seeds	oil

Sieve the gram flour into a large bowl, stir in the remaining ingredients, add I tablespoon of oil, and then beat in about 250ml of cold water to form a thick pouring batter. Leave to settle for about 15 minutes.

Brush an 18cm heavy-based non-stick frying pan or pancake pan with a little oil.

Pour in a large spoonful of the batter, tilting it to coat the whole pan, and cook on medium heat for about 2 minutes. Carefully turn over, add ½ teaspoon of oil and cook for about another 2 minutes. Repeat the process to make 5 more pancakes.

These pancakes can be prepared earlier, wrapped in foil and re-heated in a hot oven just before serving.

Cabbage, Carrot and Mango Relish

This very quick, nutritious and colourful relish can be served on its own, hot or cold, or as a stuffing for the Indian pancake.

Serves 4 - 6

1 ½ teaspoons oil
½ teaspoon cumin seeds
100g white cabbage - shredded
1 carrot - cut into matchsticks
1 long green chilli - de-seeded and
   quartered lengthways

1 small unripe mango - skinned and sliced into matchsticks
salt to taste
½ teaspoon sugar
½ teaspoon chilli powder
lime juice to taste

- Warm the oil in a wok or a large frying pan and add the cumin seeds, vegetables and mango. Stir-fry for a few minutes.

- Add the salt, sugar, chilli powder and lime juice, and stir-fry for 4-5 minutes. Serve hot or cold.

- To serve – put a big spoonful of the relish on the pancake and roll like a swiss-roll before serving.

Red Cabbage Coleslaw

The combination of slightly bitter red cabbage and the sweetness of the beetroot makes a wonderful salad. Use a mandolin grater to shred the vegetables.

Serves 8 - 10

2 handfuls finely shredded red cabbage
2 handfuls finely shredded carrot
2 handfuls finely shredded cucumber
2 handfuls finely shredded raw beetroot
2 handfuls finely sliced celeriac
1 handful finely sliced red onion
1 handful flat leaf parsley leaves

Dressing:
150g natural yogurt (small packet)
salt to taste
1 teaspoon cumin seeds - roasted
½ teaspoon red chilli powder or
  1 teaspoon Harissa paste
  (hot chilli Moroccan paste)

- Mix all the ingredients for the dressing in a bowl.

- In a serving bowl, mix the finely shredded red cabbage, carrot, cucumber, beetroot, celeriac and red onion.

- Drizzle the dressing on this coleslaw and mix well. Garnish with parsley.

- Let the salad marinate in the dressing before serving.

- Mix and match the above ingredients to your preference.

* To roast cumin seeds, dry-roast the seeds in a non-stick frying pan without any oil until lightly brown.

Stir Fry Chinese Cabbage and Kohlrabi with Walnut Dressing

Chinese cabbage, found in oriental shops and some supermarkets, is rich in nutrients. One cup of chopped Chinese cabbage contains nearly the entire RDA for antioxidant beta carotene (which the body can convert to vitamin A as needed). It also has antioxidant vitamin C, potassium and calcium.

Kohlrabi contains antioxidant vitamin C, potassium and antioxidant vitamin E. It is very versatile as it can be eaten steamed, served hot as a side dish, or is ideal for a crunchy stir-fry.

Serves 4

> 1 cup finely shredded Chinese cabbage
> 1 kohlrabi
> 2 tablespoons walnut oil or olive oil
> handful of flat leaf parsley
> handful of walnuts
> handful of sliced sun dried tomatoes or cherry tomatoes
> salt and lime juice to taste
> lettuce leaves or baby cos lettuce

- Finely shred the Chinese cabbage.

- Peel the kohlrabi and slice it finely – similar to the shredded cabbage.

- In a wok, add 2 tablespoons of walnut oil or olive oil. Stir fry the cabbage and kohlrabi for 4-6 minutes. Add a handful of chopped flat leaf parsley and walnuts.

- Season with salt, and lime juice.

- Decorate with slices of sun dried tomatoes or cherry tomatoes. Serve on a bed of baby cos lettuce or mixed lettuce leaves.

Chapter 2

Introduction	26
Kale Soup with Broccoli	27
Good Food Salad	30
Pesto Pasta Salad	31
Chinese Style Ginger Pak Choi	32
Spicy Fenugreek and Coriander Fritters	33
Spinach, Fennel, Orange and Roasted Nut Salad with Oriental Dressing	35
Stir-Fried Spinach Curry	36
Spinach and Feta Parcels	37
Green Risotto with Courgette and Tomato Salsa	39

Leafy Greens

Introduction

Leafy green vegetables like spinach, kale, rocket leaves, watercress, pak choi and most green herbs, such as coriander, methi (fenugreek), parsley and mint are packed with phytochemicals like caretonoids, folate, vitamin C, vitamin K and fibre. Many studies show that these phytochemicals delay the ageing process. They are also a good source of calcium and help to protect against osteoporosis.

The risk of heart disease can be reduced by eating a lot of greens. They contain the phytonutrient **folate**, which is a member of the vitamin B group. (Folate is often referred to as folic acid which is a manufactured form of the vitamin). Folate can help to regulate blood levels of homocysteine, which is a by product of protein metabolism in the body. An increased level of homocysteine can lead to the development of atherosclerosis and heart disease. Folate is needed for the absorption of iron and is also necessary for the production of DNA. Birth defects such as spina bifida have been linked with low levels of folate in early stages of pregnancy. It is important for anyone trying to get pregnant to eat lots of greens.

Most of the fibre found in *leafy greens* is soluble fibre which dissolves in water and passes through the digestive system much more slowly than insoluble fibre. **Soluble fibre** as it moves down the digestive system can help to reduce and remove blood lipids like triglycerides and cholesterol

and also helps to stabilise blood sugar, which is helpful for people who have diabetes.

The first recipe in this chapter has to be *Kale Soup with Broccoli* which are both star vegetables, the addition of a few spices add a zing to the strong kale flavour. I hope the list of goodness in the ingredients of the *Good Food Salad* are impressive enough to convince you to eat this at least twice a week. Get into the habit of eating a bowl of greens, raw as a salad for lunch or before a main meal every day to obtain the maximum benefits of its phytonutrients – boiling the leafy greens for very long can destroy a lot of the folate content of the food. The tempting recipes for *Spinach Curry, Green Risotto* and *Fenugreek Fritters* will hopefully inspire you to eat greens regularly.

Pak Choi

Kale Soup with Broccoli

One cup of kale has almost twice the RDA of the antioxidant beta carotene (which the body can convert to vitamin A as needed) and is a rich source of antioxidants vitamin C and vitamin E. Kale is one of the best sources of carotenoids, lutein and zeaxanthin, both help to absorb the harmful blue light from the sun's rays which can damage the central region of the retina at the back of the eye and this can lead to macular degeneration.

Kale - this robust, nutritious green vegetable is also a rich source of a form of calcium which is easily absorbed by the body, this calcium helps to strengthen bones. Kale contains potassium which helps maintain normal blood pressure while the fibre content protects against cancer. The sulforaphane and indoles in kale stimulate the body to produce cancer-fighting enzymes.

What more do you need?! Kale soup with the superstar vegetable broccoli. Small, raw broccoli florets added at the last minute, gently cook as the soup is heated and acts as a garnish. This way none of the nutrients of broccoli are lost in the cooking process. This novel idea of mine using broccoli florets as a garnish works very well.

Serves 4 - 6

1 packet kale (approx 200g)	1 teaspoon caraway seeds
1 tablespoon olive oil	1 teaspoon coriander seeds
1 small sweet potato - cubed	1 teaspoon cumin seeds
1 red onion – cubed	2 handfuls broccoli florets
725ml water or stock	seasoning–salt, pepper, lime juice

- In a large pan, warm the oil and add caraway, coriander, cumin seeds and onion. Sauté for 3 minutes. Add the sweet potato, kale leaves and the water or vegetable stock. Cook for 20 minutes. Liquidise the soup using a hand blender.

- Season well using a little salt, freshly ground black pepper and lime juice. Add the finely sliced broccoli florets five minute before serving. Serve the soup hot. (Add extra water if you want a thinner consistency). Sieve the soup if you prefer it silky smooth.

- This soup is excellent served with a dollop of sour cream or a few drops of a good lemon flavoured olive oil.

* If kale is not readily available, spinach can be used for the soup, especially for children who prefer the silky texture of spinach to kale. Kale could also be stir-fried in olive oil and sesame seeds to serve as a side dish.

Good Food Salad Ingredients

All the ingredients of this star food salad are full of phytonutrients and eating it on a regular basis will provide lots of energy and vitality. The salad looks good, tastes good and will surely make you feel good.

Below are the nutritional reasons for the combination of various *Good Food Salad* ingredients.

Parsley The combination of both the iron and vitamin C in parsley, helps the iron to be absorbed more easily from the food. Parsley is a diuretic, it can help to remove excess water from the body. Parsley helps the adrenal gland and thyroid gland to function, and it contains compounds called courmarins which are natural blood thinners, excellent for cardiovascular health. I use flat leaf parsley not only as a garnish but as a main ingredient in lots of my dishes.

Mint is a great breath freshener, rich in folate and mint gives a unique kick to the salad.

Coriander is anti-viral and helps to get rid of heavy metals such as mercury and lead from the body.

Watercress has the antioxidant beta carotene which is converted into vitamin A by the body and it has the carotenoids lutein and zeaxanthin which are great for healthy skin and eyes. Watercress also has vitamin C, calcium, iron and most B vitamins (including folate) and iodine. Watercress has a rich source of glucosinolates, sulphur containing water soluble phytochemicals, which are converted to

isothiocyanates. Research suggests these can inhibit cancer development. It also has the powerful antioxidant quercetin, a type of flavonoid found in red onions and watermelons. As a vegetable, watercress is very high on the **ORAC score** (ORAC score is a measure of the food's antioxidant value).

Quinoa is rich in all 8 essential amino acids, which makes it a "complete protein". It is also an excellent source of potassium, iron, zinc and vitamin B and it has a lot of fibre.

Alfalfa is an anti-inflammatory food, very rich in chlorophyll and is a diuretic food. It helps to lower blood pressure and is rich in vitamins and minerals. Alfalfa sprouts are available from health stores and specialty shops.

Cucumber is one of the oldest known vegetables, it is diuretic (which helps prevent water retention) and its skin contains a compound called sterol which helps to lower cholesterol.

Avocado is a star food, although one tends to think of it as fattening, it is cholesterol free and it contains lots of good monounsaturated fat which helps to reduce LDL (bad cholesterol). It also contains vitamin E and fibre. Try to eat a small avocado at least four times a week.

Tomatoes contain a powerful phytochemical called lycopene, a member of the carotenoid family. Lycopene is thought to help reduce the risk of prostate cancer. Most of the antioxidants are under the skin of a fruit or vegetable, so do not peel the fruit or vegetable unless necessary. To obtain maximum antioxidants, try to use cherry tomatoes which have more skin than pulp. (I often use cherry tomatoes in my curries as they stay intact and look good).

Walnuts out of all the nuts, have the highest overall antioxidant activity - ORAC (Oxygen Radical Absorption Capacity). Walnuts are one of the few sources of plant-derived omega 3 essential fatty acids - which helps thin the blood (helps the blood to flow freely and prevents clots from forming), lowers blood pressure and have anti-inflammatory properties.

Olive Oil is very high in monounsaturated fat which helps to lower the bad LDL cholesterol (low density lipoprotein), without lowering the good HDL cholesterol (high density lipoprotein). Latest research has shown that eating a Mediterranean diet and cooking with olive oil may help to prevent Alzheimer's disease and risk of heart attack.

Lime contains vitamin C which is an antioxidant and a few drops of lime added to food lowers its GI (glycemic index). Low GI foods provide slow released energy which is excellent for diabetics. The GI index relates only to carbohydrates (which are starchy and sweet foods), and is a way of ranking foods based on the rate at which they raise blood glucose levels.

Good Food Salad

Serves 6

    1 bunch flat leaf parsley
    ½ bunch mint
    ½ bunch coriander
    1 bunch watercress
    3 handfuls of alfalfa sprouts (if available)
    4 full tablespoons quinoa (or cracked wheat or couscous)
    2 small cucumbers
    1 big avocado
    1 packet cherry tomatoes – approx 15
    approx 100g walnut pieces or other nuts
    2-3 tablespoons olive oil
    1 fresh lime
    salt and freshly ground black pepper to taste

- Wash all the leafy green ingredients well and cut into bite size pieces.

- Wash the quinoa and soak it for 20 minutes, then cook the quinoa in 600ml of water until the grains open (approx 10-12 minutes). Strain it and let it cool.

- Chop the cucumber, avocado, tomatoes and walnuts into bite size pieces.

- Mix all the above ingredients in a salad bowl. Drizzle the olive oil and lime juice over the salad and season to taste.

- Mix and match the above ingredients to your preference.

* You can make the *Good Food Salad* into a main meal, full of essential goodness, by adding a few stir fried tofu pieces and a slice of baked butternut squash.

Pesto Pasta Salad

My daughter Lavina created this exciting combination of pasta salad for a Sunday lunch and I could not help but include it for its super goodness. It's an ideal cold salad dish for summer parties. As an alternative to the pesto recipe below if you are short of time, use a good quality Italian ready-made pesto.

Serves 6 - 8

4 handfuls dry pasta – fusilli or bowtie shapes
100g fine green beans
half bunch watercress – leaves only
2 handfuls black olives
2 handfuls feta cheese - cubed
2 tablespoons pine nuts
juice and the zest of one small lime
salt and freshly ground black pepper to taste
2 tablespoons good quality olive oil

For pesto
2 handfuls each of basil leaves, rocket and watercress
1 tablespoon olive oil
1 tablespoon pine nuts
1 teaspoon lime juice
pinch of salt

- Boil the pasta according to the instructions on the packet, drain and cool.

- Par boil green beans in boiling water for 4 minutes, drain and cool under cold water. Cut into bite size pieces. (Alternatively steam the beans till tender).

- De-stone the black olives and slice.

- Cube the feta cheese.

- Dry roast 2 tablespoons pine nuts in a small non-stick frying pan until golden.

- For the pesto, blend basil, rocket, watercress, olive oil, pine nuts and lime juice in a food processor and season well.

- In a big salad bowl, mix together the pasta, green beans, watercress leaves, olives, feta cheese, pine nuts, lime juice and lime zest.

- Mix in the prepared pesto and two tablespoons of olive oil, season if necessary.

  * You can add one clove of garlic to the above pesto for extra flavour.
  Use any left over pesto on warm steamed new potatoes for a treat.

Chinese Style Ginger Pak Choi

Serve this hot as part of a Chinese meal or cold with a green salad.

Serves 2 - 4

6 florets of pak choi
1 tablespoon oil
1 inch piece of ginger
½ long red chilli
1-2 garlic cloves (finely sliced) optional
1 tablespoon light soya sauce
2 tablespoons toasted flaked almonds

- Cut the pak choi into bite size pieces. If using baby pak choi leave it whole.

- Skin the ginger and cut into small slices like matchsticks. Chop the red chilli into tiny pieces.

- In a wok, warm the oil, add the ginger and stir-fry for a minute.

- Add the pak choi, chilli, garlic, soya sauce, 3 tablespoons of water and cook for 2-3 minutes.

- Sprinkle with flaked almonds. Serve hot or cold.

* The same recipe can be made using tender **stem broccoli** which provides more nutrients than mature broccoli – steam or par boil the tender stem broccoli for 2-3 minutes before stir frying.

Pak Choi

Spicy Fenugreek and Coriander Fritters

Fenugreek (small-leafed Indian spinach known as methi), has been eaten in India since ancient times both as food and medicine. Research suggests that the fenugreek seeds have antibiotic, anti-ulcer and anti-cancer properties. It is most effective in lowering blood glucose so it is good for anyone with type 2 diabetes. It also helps to lower blood pressure and prevent gas in the intestine i.e. it's good for digestion. Fenugreek contains selenium and is a good source of phytoestrogens, a very useful spice/herb for women - possibly helping to reduce the discomfort of the menopause. Fresh fenugreek bunches are available from Asian stores and major supermarkets.

Makes 12 - 16 Fritters

4 handfuls fenugreek leaves – discard the big stems
4 handfuls coriander leaves
100g gram flour
½ green chilli – finely sliced
1 teaspoon cumin seeds
1 teaspoon coriander seeds

½ teaspoon fenugreek seeds
½ teaspoon whole black pepper
1 teaspoon salt or less
1 teaspoon lime juice
1 teaspoon oil
¼ teaspoon baking powder
extra oil for frying

- Wash fenugreek and coriander leaves and chop finely. Finely slice the green chilli (add more green chilli if you like it hot).

- In a pestle and mortar or a spice grinder, coarsely grind the cumin, coriander, fenugreek and black pepper seeds together.

- In a jug or a bowl, mix 100g gram flour and 100ml cold water – use a whisk or a hand blender and mix it well to form a smooth batter. Add the grounded cumin, coriander, fenugreek and black pepper into the batter.

- Add the fenugreek, coriander, chilli, lime juice, 1 teaspoon oil and ¼ teaspoon baking powder to the gram flour mix, season to taste with salt.

- Deep fry the fritters till golden (use a dessertspoon to drop the mixture in hot oil). Complete the frying in 2-3 batches, depending on the size of the pan. (These fritters can also be shallow fried in a non-stick frying pan).

- Drain the fritters on kitchen paper and serve hot.

  * Spicy Tomato Salsa (page 43) is ideal as a dip for these fritters.

Spinach, Fennel, Orange and Roasted Nut Salad with Oriental Dressing

This is a colourful combination of spinach, fennel and orange. The oriental dressing gives it a fresh flavour, and it can be assembled instantly.

Serves 4 - 6

4 handfuls baby spinach
2 fennel bulbs
2 oranges
2 handfuls roasted cashew nuts or macadamia nuts

For the Dressing:
2 tablespoons soya sauce
1 tablespoon toasted sesame oil
1 tablespoon rice vinegar (or lime juice)
salt to taste

- Wash the baby spinach well and pat dry with kitchen paper.

- Slice the fennel bulbs into fine segments.

- Remove the skin of the oranges; use a sharp knife to slice between the segments (keep the orange segments whole.)

- Roast the nuts in a warm oven until golden.

- Combine all the ingredients of the dressing in a jar and season to taste.

- Mix the spinach, fennel, oranges and nuts with the dressing just before serving.

Spinach, Fennel, Orange and Roasted Nut Salad with Oriental Dressing

Fennel

Stir-Fried Spinach Curry

Spinach is a star food with its high content of antioxidant carotenoids (lutein and zeaxanthin) which can protect the eyes. Research studies have shown that a higher intake of foods rich in these carotenoids, especially spinach, kale, spring greens, watercress and yellow foods, for example corn and orange peppers, have been associated with a lower incidence of eye diseases such as cataract and age-related macular degeneration, the most common cause of poor vision and blindness in people over 60 in the UK. It also contains the two most important antioxidants, glutathione and alpha lipoic acid, which help to protect DNA, boost the immune system, detoxify pollutants and reduce chronic inflammation.

Spinach is an excellent source of folate, potassium, magnesium and calcium which all help to prevent cardio vascular diseases, and it contains vitamin K which is necessary for proper blood coagulation.

Only one word of caution, spinach contains high levels of oxalates which can significantly reduce calcium bio availability and should be avoided by those suffering from kidney stones. Therefore spinach should be eaten in moderation. (Kale and watercress contain low levels of oxalates).

Serves - 4

1 x 300g packet of spinach	2 tablespoons oil
2 tablespoons gram flour	1 teaspoon cumin seeds
½ teaspoon salt	2 cloves garlic - peeled, finely sliced
½ teaspoon chilli powder	½ green chilli - chopped
2 teaspoons dhana jeera	½ teaspoon lime juice

- In a big saucepan, cook the washed spinach with the lid on for 10 minutes (do not add any water or oil, it will wilt in its own water).

- Remove the spinach, and let it cool on a strainer with a glass bowl under it. The excess water will collect in the glass bowl. Make it up to 200ml by adding extra water. Add 2 tablespoons of gram flour, salt, red chilli powder and dhana jeera to this water – stir well.

- In a non-stick wok, warm 2 tablespoons of oil, add the cumin seeds and mix in the sliced garlic and the cooked spinach. Add the chopped green chilli and the water mixture containing the gram flour and the spices.

- Stir well, cook on a medium heat for 10-12 minutes until the spinach and spices are cooked to make a soft runny curry. Season with lime juice and serve hot, as part of an Indian main meal.

Spinach and Feta Parcels

These puff pastry parcels are good for a quick and tasty light lunch or serve as a starter to any main meal. Use ready rolled chilled puff pastry available in major supermarkets. This is a variation of the traditional Greek dish which uses filo pastry.

Makes 14 Parcels

1 packet puff pastry	*Seasoning:*
1 tablespoon olive oil	very little salt to taste
1 teaspoon caraway seeds	freshly ground pepper
1 bag fresh spinach – approx 450g	freshly ground nutmeg
200g feta cheese	

- Unroll the sheet of puff pastry on a cool surface and leave for 20 minutes. Pre-heat the oven to 220°C, 425°F, Gas Mark 7.

- Wash the spinach thoroughly in cold water, cut it into big bite size pieces.

- In a big saucepan, add one tablespoon of olive oil, the caraway seeds and the spinach. Cook until spinach has wilted (5-7 minutes).

- Strain the spinach well to remove any excess water. Let it dry and cool a little and mix in the seasonings – salt, pepper and nutmeg.

- Crumble in the feta cheese and mix it well together so that the cheese and the spinach are thoroughly blended.

- Roll out the pastry a little thinner and cut lengthways in the middle, into 2 sections, and again cut the sections into 7 portions each – which gives 14 pastry pieces. Stuff each pastry piece with a little of the spinach mixture, seal the edges using a fork, use a pair of scissors to cut a little slit on each pastry for steam to escape and bake until beautifully golden, approximately 12 minutes.

* To serve as a main meal:
Accompany these parcels with steamed broccoli, oven baked sweet potato chips (page 73) and roasted tomato and red pepper soup (page 45). Use less stock to cook this soup, so it stays thick and can be used as a dip for parcels.

* Use the excess water from the cooked spinach as a stock for soup - keeps in the fridge for 2 days.

Green Risotto with Courgette and Tomato Salsa

Risotto is one of my favourite "comfort foods" and it takes very little time to create this stunning presentation.

Serves - 2

150g risotto rice
1-2 tablespoons olive oil
600ml vegetable stock (approx)
3 spring onion stalks - chopped
1 clove garlic - chopped
2 handfuls of greens: a combination of baby spinach, watercress and rocket
1 courgette (long and straight)
1 tablespoon grated parmesan or cheddar cheese

some extra cheese for garnish
seasoning – salt and lime juice to taste

For the Tomato Salsa:
10 cherry tomatoes – cut in half
salt and pepper to taste
2 teaspoons balsamic vinegar
10 fresh basil leaves

- Chop the spinach, watercress and rocket leaves in a food processor.

- In a saucepan, boil the vegetable stock (homemade stock or use 2 teaspoons of Marigold Swiss bouillon powder in 600ml water) then lower the heat and simmer it.

- In another saucepan, warm the olive oil, sauté the chopped spring onion and garlic for 2 minutes. Add the rice, stir to coat well until the rice is translucent. Cook on moderate heat.

- Add the hot stock, one ladle full at a time, let the rice absorb it before adding more stock, stir after each addition till three quarters of the stock has been added to the rice.

- Add the chopped greens to the rice and mix well. Keep on adding the hot stock until the risotto is creamy and the rice has a slight bite. Stir in the cheese and lime juice and season well.

- Slice the courgette lengthways. Spread a little olive oil on the courgette slices and chargrill on both sides (using a chargrill pan or a non-stick pan).

- Prepare the tomato salsa by mixing the tomato pieces, salt, pepper, balsamic vinegar and basil leaves in a bowl.

To serve the risotto in style:
Use a 9cm metal ring mould and place the courgette slices against the inside of the mould. Fill it well with the warm green risotto. Remove the mould. Serve immediately with the tomato salsa around the green risotto and a slice of parmesan cheese.

Spinach, fennel, orange and roasted nut salad
Green Risotto with Courgette and Tomato Salsa

Chapter 3

Introduction   42

Spicy Tomato Salsa   43

Roasted Tomato and Red Pepper Soup   45

Tomato and Garlic Bruschetta   47

Tomato and Avocado Raita   48

Penne Arrabiata   49

Tomatoes Baked with Herb Pesto   51

Tomato, Onion and Potato Gratin with Oregano   52

Tomato and Green Pepper Curry   53

Tomatoes

Introduction

Tomatoes, an integral part of the Mediterranean diet, contain a powerful phyto-chemical called **lycopene** (a member of the carotenoid family) which gives tomatoes a red colour. Over the past decade, mounting evidence suggests that the consumption of fresh and processed tomato products is associated with a reduced risk of prostate cancer. Latest research also finds that lycopene helps to protect the skin from damaging UV radiation from the sun. The tomatoes are also an excellent source of nutrients including fibre, polyphenols, antioxidant carotenoids, folate, antioxidant vitamin C and potassium as well as some antioxidant vitamin E. It is the **synergy** of all these nutrients and lycopene which makes tomatoes a star food – try to eat **tomatoes daily** to maximise the lycopene content in the body.

Cooking and processing tomatoes increases the lycopene content and heat changes the chemical structure of lycopene, making it easy for the body to absorb it. The convenient staple tomato ketchup, a popular choice for children, tomato puree and tinned tomatoes are all rich sources of lycopene. When serving raw tomatoes always drizzle a little olive oil over them for maximum lycopene absorption by the body – *lycopene is fat soluble* or eat some avocado, cheese or nuts with the raw tomatoes, the oil in these foods will help the lycopene to be absorbed easily.

You will notice the use of tomatoes throughout most of the relevant recipes in this book – a reflection of my addiction to tomatoes.

The French refer to the tomato as a "love apple" and in my view to love oneself, "eating a few tomatoes a day can be celebrated as a cancer free day".

Spicy Tomato Salsa

This versatile tomato salsa is ideal as a dip or serve it with any Indian meal. It keeps for 2 days in the fridge.

Serves 2 - 4

2 big ripe tomatoes - skinned
1 shallot or small onion
½ red chilli - de-seeded
5cm piece of cucumber
5cm piece of carrot
½ teaspoon salt
1 teaspoon lime juice

- Mix all the above ingredients in a food processor and blend until everything is finely chopped. Add extra red chilli if you like it hot.

- Store the salsa in a glass jar.

Tomatoes

Roasted Tomato and Red Pepper Soup

The health benefits of tomatoes and red peppers combined makes this soup the best insurance policy for good health. The roasting gives it a caramelised flavour and also concentrates the taste.

This is my favourite soup, so easy and simple - once tasted it becomes addictive. Spice it up with Tabasco and lots of fresh basil.

Serves 4

2 big red peppers
450g tomatoes
1 leek or red onion - sliced
1 - 2 tablespoons olive oil
600ml vegetable stock or water
salt to taste
freshly ground black pepper
for garnish – crème fraiche (optional)

- Pre-heat the oven to 200°C, 400°F, Gas Mark 6.

- Cut each red pepper into quarters, remove the seeds. Cut the tomatoes in half. Place the tomatoes and peppers in a roasting tin.

- Drizzle 1 tablespoon of olive oil on the sliced tomatoes and peppers - roast for half an hour.

- Warm 1 tablespoon of olive oil in a big pan, and sauté the sliced leek or onion for 3 minutes. Add the above mixture and the vegetable stock (or water) and cook for 20 minutes.

- When the soup is slightly cold, liquidise the mixture thoroughly, by using a hand blender. (If you prefer it silky smooth, sieve the soup through a big holed soup sieve after liquidising.)

- Season to taste. Serve the soup hot, garnished with crème fraiche (optional), and a slice of good bread. (e.g. cinnamon spiced nut bread page 130).

Roasted Tomato and Red Pepper Soup

Tomato and Garlic Bruschetta

The substance allicin, which gives garlic its distinctive aroma, has antibiotic and antifungal properties. Garlic is a good source of vitamin B, zinc and antioxidant vitamin C, which all helps to boost the immune system. Research studies suggest that to obtain the full benefit of allicin, the garlic needs to be eaten raw, so for maximum benefit, spread loads of garlic on bruschetta.

Makes 6 - 8 slices

1 ciabatta bread or any Italian bread	salt – to taste
20 cherry tomatoes or more	freshly ground black pepper
4-6 cloves of garlic	extra virgin olive oil
handful basil	3 tablespoons balsamic vinegar

- Cut the tomatoes into bite size pieces. Mix in a little olive oil, balsamic vinegar, chopped basil, and season to taste.

- Use a griddle pan to grill the bread slice until just golden. (Cut a thick slice of the bread and drizzle a little olive oil over it before grilling.) – Alternatively, toast the slice of bread in a hot oven for a few minutes.

- Rub the toasted bread slice with a halved fresh garlic clove.

- Serve drizzled with extra virgin olive oil and topped with the tomato mixture. Repeat with extra slices of bread as required.

- For an extra burst of flavour serve with oven roasted cherry tomatoes and pesto (see recipe for Tomatoes Baked with Herb Pesto on page 51).

Tomato and garlic bruschetta is an easy, tasty, refreshing starter. For garlic lovers, sliced garlic can be mixed in with the tomato mixture.

* **Two alternative versions:**
Wild mushroom bruschetta - Stir fry sliced wild mushrooms in olive oil, one clove of garlic, one shallot and herbs. Serve on a toasted garlicky bruschetta slice, with oven roasted cherry tomatoes.

Goats' cheese and roasted cherry tomato bruschetta – Roast cherry tomatoes with olive oil in a warm oven for 20 minutes. Season with rock salt and fresh basil leaves. Toast a bread slice with garlic as above. Spread it with goats' cheese and serve with oven roasted cherry tomatoes.

Tomato and Garlic Bruschetta

Tomato and Avocado Raita

Raita is a yogurt dip. This unique mixture of tomato, avocado and yogurt, the three most healthy ingredients, results in a very fresh and finger licking raita - you will want to eat the whole lot in one go! Serve it to accompany an Indian meal or as a dip with cucumber, carrots, celery etc.

Serves 1 - 2

1 big avocado
10 cherry tomatoes - chopped
½ green chilli - de-seeded and chopped
2 spring onions – finely chopped
1 handful coriander - chopped

½ teaspoon salt
freshly ground black pepper to taste
150g natural yogurt (small packet)
½ teaspoon chilli powder

- Cut the avocado in half, keeping the shell intact. Gently scoop out the avocado flesh and cut into small cubes.

- Mix tomatoes, green chilli, spring onions, coriander, salt, pepper and yogurt together in a bowl and season to taste.

- Serve, garnished with the chilli powder, in the avocado shells or a bowl.

Avocado

Penne Arrabiata

This pasta dish is easy yet so satisfying – my grandchildren Sai, Saj and Sahil's favourite Sunday lunch.

The best tomato sauce is prepared using good quality fresh tomatoes, Italian tinned tomatoes and tomato puree. In summer, prepare the tomato sauce using only fresh ripe tomatoes and tomato puree. Also buy the best quality penne pasta and cook it al'dente.

Extra left over tomato sauce can be kept in the fridge in a glass jar for 4-6 days.

Serves 4

225g penne pasta
6 big plum or vine tomatoes - peeled
400g tin Italian plum tomatoes
1 tablespoon tomato puree
3 tablespoons olive oil
1 teaspoon salt or less to taste
1 teaspoon sugar

2 cloves garlic
½ teaspoon red chilli flakes
½ red chilli – chopped (optional)
1 tablespoon flat leaf parsley
2 handfuls of parmesan or cheddar cheese

- Cook the pasta in a pan of boiling water, according to the instructions on the packet. Drain well.

- Meanwhile, prepare the tomato sauce. To peel away the skin of the tomato, the best method is to score the round end of the tomato with a sharp knife, place it in a bowl of boiling water for 30 seconds, remove and cool the tomato; the skin will peel off easily. Peel the skin off all the tomatoes for the sauce.

- In a blender, chop the fresh tomatoes and the tinned tomatoes to a smooth mixture. In a big saucepan add this mixture and the tomato puree with 1 tablespoon olive oil, salt and sugar. Cook the sauce covered for 15-20 minutes.

- To serve: In a wok or a pan, add 2 tablespoons of olive oil, chopped garlic, chilli flakes and finely chopped red chilli. Cook for 1 minute. Add the pasta, mix well and stir in the tomato sauce as required. Season well.

- Serve with chopped parsley and grated cheese. Accompany this dish with crusty bread to mop up the juices.

* For extra flavour, add sundried tomatoes and pitted black olives.

Tomatoes Baked with Herb Pesto

A simple yet exciting Mediterranean starter or side dish, excellent with Italian bread.

Serves 3 - 4

6 medium tomatoes
extra olive oil for cooking

Pesto:
2 cloves garlic
1 handful of rocket leaves
1 handful of basil

1 handful of mint
1 handful of flat leaf parsley
2 tablespoons olive oil
salt and freshly ground black pepper
    to taste
1 handful of pine nuts – toasted

- Pre-heat the oven to 200°C, 400°F, gas mark 6.

- Wash the tomatoes and slice the top of each tomato (save the tops as covers for baking). Carefully remove the inside seeds using a teaspoon. Arrange the tomatoes in a small oven proof dish.

- In a blender, add the garlic and the washed rocket, basil, mint, parsley and enough olive oil to make a chunky pesto.

- Place a tablespoon of this pesto in each tomato case. Season with salt and pepper. Arrange the cut slices of tomato on top of each stuffed tomato. Drizzle a little olive oil on all the tomatoes and bake for 30 minutes until the tomatoes are soft.

- Serve topped with toasted pine nuts and all the juices from the baking dish.
  This dish can be served hot or cold as a side dish.

* If you like cheese, add 2 tablespoons of grated parmesan cheese to the herb pesto.

* Tomatoes baked with herb pesto can also be served on a bed of cooked couscous or cooked brown rice.

Tomatoes Baked with Herb Pesto

Tomato, Onion and Potato Gratin with Oregano

This unusual baked dish is a good accompaniment to an Italian pasta dish.
Oregano has been used for many years as a treatment for respiratory ailments. It contains anti-inflammatory compounds which have protective effects against chronic diseases. It is commonly used in the Mediterranean diet.

Onions contain flavonoids which help fight cancers, and red onions and shallots contain a powerful antioxidant, called quercetin.

Serves 2 - 4

2 large baking potatoes
1 large onion
400g tin Italian plum tomatoes
3 tablespoons olive oil
2 teaspoons dry oregano (Italian herb)
salt and freshly ground black pepper
    to taste

- Pre-heat the oven to 200°C, 400°F, Gas Mark 6.

- Thinly slice the potatoes into discs and either steam or par boil for a few minutes.

- Peel the onion and slice, into rings. Slice the plum tomatoes, reserving the juice.

- Lightly oil a shallow oven dish and arrange thin layers of potatoes, onions and tomatoes with some tomato juice. Season with olive oil, salt, pepper and oregano. Repeat with the remaining potatoes, onions and tomato. Cover the oven dish with aluminium foil.

- Bake in a moderately hot oven until soft for approximately 30-40 minutes.

- Serve as a side dish with pasta or a green salad.

Tomato and Green Pepper Curry

The combination of the red tomatoes and green peppers makes a colourful and tasty dish. It is a quick and easy curry to cook for complete beginners. Serve it with rice or naan bread.

Serves 2

1 big green pepper
225g tomatoes
2 tablespoons oil
1 teaspoon cumin seeds
1 teaspoon salt or less
$\frac{1}{2}$ teaspoon chilli powder

$\frac{1}{4}$ teaspoon turmeric
1 tablespoon dhana jeera
$\frac{1}{2}$ teaspoon garam masala
4 tablespoons tinned coconut milk
a few fresh coriander leaves

- Wash and de-seed the green pepper and cut it into big chunks. Cut the tomatoes into equal-sized chunks.

- Warm the oil in a saucepan, add the cumin seeds and green pepper. Sauté for 2-3 minutes and add the tomatoes. Cook for 5 minutes.

- Add the salt, chilli powder, turmeric, dhana jeera, and garam masala, one by one. Simmer covered, for 7 minutes, adding the coconut milk for the last 5 minutes.

- Garnish with the coriander leaves and serve.

* Add extra coconut milk to gain a consistency that is somewhere between a curry and a dal.

Tomato

Chapter 4

Introduction   56

Roasted Tofu with Spring Onion and
Cashew Nuts   57

Golden Tofu with Coconut Curry Sauce   58

Spicy Soya Bean Curry   59

Chilli Tofu   61

Soya Bean Pods - Edamame   62

Soya Milk   62

Soya Flour   62

Soya
Beans

Lemon Grass, Green Chillies,
Red Chillies, Lime Leaves

Introduction

Often referred to as the "miracle beans", soya beans are a good source of protein for vegetarians as they contain all the essential amino acids. They are also rich in fibre, important B vitamins, calcium, iron and zinc. The soya beans are a plant source of omega 3 essential fatty acid, which is helpful in the prevention of heart disease and cancer. Soya bean products, are rich in **isoflavones,** compounds that are phytoestrogens, which are naturally occurring plant substances with a chemical structure very similar to our own hormone oestrogen. One of the most widely researched isoflavones is genistein, which binds to the oestrogen receptors alpha and beta and might play a role in delaying and preventing hormone related cancers. Isoflavones may help to reduce the discomfort of menopause.

There is a lot of controversy on all the benefits of soya products but I still feel one should eat it regularly especially for its protein and isoflavones. The present research study provides modest support for the preventative role of soya against stomach cancer and heart disease. Remember to eat your soya products (tofu, soya bean, soya flour, soya milk) to get the benefits of soya phytonutrients, do not take soya supplements which may provide too many phytoestrogens and have a negative effect.

Soya tofu is bland in taste so I have spiced it up to give flavour and hope those of you who have never liked it before give it another

Red Chillies

chance. The Golden Tofu Curry is so tasty that you forget you are even eating tofu. In this country fresh tofu is available from most supermarkets and so are most of the Chinese ingredients – the main benefits of Chinese stir fry method is its versatility and ease. Sometimes I feel it is fresher, easier and more enjoyable to cook your own Chinese dishes than ringing for a "take-away". I believe in eating vegetarian foods from different cuisines and cultures, as it introduces new ingredients and tastes, thus broadening horizons for a more sophisticated palate.

Coconut

Roasted Tofu with Spring Onion and Cashew Nuts

Serves 2 - 4

400g fresh tofu - cut into 2.5cm cubes

2 tablespoons oil

1 handful cashew nuts

1 clove garlic – sliced finely

1 inch piece ginger – sliced finely

2 bunches spring onion – cut into rings

1 red chilli – de-seeded and sliced

½ lime

1-2 tablespoons soya sauce

1 tablespoon red chilli garlic sauce
(ready made in a jar)

Pre-heat the oven to 200°C, 400°F, Gas Mark 6.

Cut the tofu into small cubes and drain well.

Brush a little oil on all the tofu pieces, place in a baking dish and roast for 15-20 minutes until crisp and golden (shake all the tofu pieces half way through baking for even cooking).
In a separate baking dish, dry-roast the cashew nuts in the oven for a few minutes until golden.

In a wok, add the remaining oil and stir fry the garlic, ginger, spring onion and chilli for 4-5 minutes. Add one tablespoon of ready-made chilli garlic sauce to give extra flavour. Season well with soya sauce and lime juice.

To serve, arrange the roasted tofu in a serving dish and spoon the spiced sauce over it. Garnish with the roasted cashew nuts.

Golden Tofu with Coconut Curry Sauce

For a taste of the Orient, serve this Thai-style tofu dish with noodles or Quinoa (page 76). It is quick and easy if you have all the ingredients ready to cook and it combines two nutritious ingredients, tofu and coconut.

Latest research acknowledges coconut as the new star food. Coconut oil is a natural source of medium and short chain fatty acids. It contains lauric acid, caprylic acid and capric acid which all have antibacterial, anti-viral and anti-fungal properties, this gives it the incredible health promoting properties. Coconut is saturated fat but chemically it is very stable and is not oxidised easily. Research shows that it is so resistant to free radical attack that it acts as an antioxidant.

Serves 2 - 4

400g tofu – cut into 2.5cm cubes	*Seasoning:*
2 ½ tablespoons groundnut oil	2 tablespoons light soya sauce
1 small red onion – finely sliced	2 teaspoons light brown sugar
1 clove garlic – chopped	2 teaspoons lime juice
½ red chilli – de-seeded and sliced	2 teaspoons chilli sauce
half a red pepper – finely sliced	2 teaspoons curry powder
1 inch piece ginger – finely sliced	salt to taste
2 lightly crushed stems of lemon grass	2 fresh lime leaves (optional)
150ml coconut milk – or more to taste	
1 large handful coriander leaves	
50g salted peanuts – coarsely chopped	

Cut the tofu into cubes. Ideally keep the tofu cubes in a strainer for half an hour and drain well, but if you are in a hurry, drain the tofu and pat-dry with kitchen paper before cooking to remove excess water.

In a non-stick frying pan, sauté the tofu in 1 tablespoon oil until golden (approx 5-7 minutes).

Meanwhile, in a wok or a big saucepan add 1 ½ tablespoons oil, sauté the onion for 3 minutes, add garlic, chilli, red pepper, ginger and the lemon grass sticks. Stir fry for another 5 minutes, then add the soya sauce, brown sugar, lime juice, chilli sauce, curry powder and salt to taste.

Add the golden tofu to this mixture. Mix well. Add the coconut milk and lime leaves (are very fragrant) and cook covered on medium heat for 10 minutes. Remove the lemon grass stems.

Garnish with coriander leaves and chopped peanuts, before serving.

Spicy Soya Bean Curry

Soya beans are rich in lecithin and research suggests that lecithin breaks up cholesterol into small particles, which the body can dispose of easily, thus helping to reduce cholesterol levels. Recent research also suggests that lecithin may help to delay the ageing process by helping to rebuild new cells in the body.

Soya beans are available fresh and frozen from major supermarkets and a quick, easy and tasty curry can be prepared with the addition of spices.

Steamed soya beans are very handy, taste good and look stunning. The beans can be added to pasta dishes, any green salad, especially my Good Food Salad (page 30) or used as a side vegetable – an ideal way to take soya protein.

Serves 2 - 4

1 tablespoon oil	1 teaspoon salt
1 teaspoon cumin seeds	½ teaspoon chilli powder
225g soya beans	½ teaspoon turmeric
3 big tomatoes – skinned and chopped	1 tablespoon dhana jeera
2 tablespoons grated coconut	

Warm the oil in a saucepan, add the cumin seeds and stir in the soya beans. Stir-fry for 2-3 minutes. Add 300ml water and let it simmer for 10 minutes, until the soya beans are tender.

Add the finely chopped tomatoes, salt, chilli powder, turmeric, dhana jeera and grated coconut (fresh or frozen coconut can be used). Cover and cook on medium heat for a further 10-15 minutes, until the sauce is thick.

Serve this curry as part of an Indian meal.

Chilli Tofu

Tofu is made from soya beans, it is a good source of protein as it contains all the essential amino acids and it provides calcium which helps strengthen the bones.

Serves 2 - 3

400g fresh tofu

2 tablespoons oil

For the chilli sauce:

1 inch ginger - finely sliced

3 garlic cloves - sliced

½ red onion – long thin slices

½ red pepper – long thin slices

½ long red chilli – finely diced

½ teaspoon salt

2 tablespoons soya sauce

1 tablespoon lime juice

2 tablespoons of ready-made
chilli garlic sauce

Cut the tofu into 2.5cm cubes. Drain well in a sieve and pat dry with kitchen paper.

In a non-stick frying pan, warm 1 tablespoon of oil and sauté the tofu cubes evenly, till golden (approx 5 minutes).

Carefully remove the tofu to a serving dish.

In the same frying pan, add a little more oil if necessary and sauté ginger, garlic, red onion, red pepper and red chilli for 5 minutes. Season with salt, soya sauce, lime juice and chilli garlic sauce.

Add the tofu pieces to the frying pan. Mix well and cook for a further 5 minutes. Serve this hot chilli tofu with Stir Fry Quinoa (page 76) or plain boiled rice.

Chilli Tofu, Stir Fry Quinoa with Pepper,
Chinese Style Ginger, Pak Choi
and Stem Brocolli

Soya Bean Pods - Edamame

Edamame, whole soya bean pods, can be bought from oriental shops and are a nutritional way of eating soya beans.

Boil or steam them in water for a few minutes, strain the pods and then toss in sea salt or Chinese mixed 5 spice. For a bit of extra heat, add some finely chopped red chilli. Serve as a starter. It is fun to suck the seeds from each cooked pod!

Soya Milk

Use soya milk instead of cow's milk to obtain the goodness of soya. It can be mixed with fresh fruits to make tasty smoothies. Silken tofu can also be added to these smoothies. I will leave this to your imagination and adventurous side - try mixing in exotic fruits like mangoes, lychees and banana.

Also try soya yogurt and soya chocolate desserts available in supermarkets and health stores. Some of these products are extremely delicious.

Soya Flour

Soya flour is rich in protein and it provides all 8 of the essential amino acids. Add it to cakes and pastry mixtures, it can also be mixed with wheat flour to prepare Indian breads like chappati and naan bread (page 121).

Selection of onions and garlic

Chapter 5

Introduction   66

Carrot, Beetroot, Apple and Turmeric Juice   67

Butternut Squash, Ginger and Cinnamon Soup   71

Oven Baked Sweet Potato Chips   73

Stuffed Mushrooms with a Medley of Coloured Peppers   74

Stir Fry Quinoa with Peppers   76

Broad Beans, Baby Asparagus and Green Beans in Mint Sauce   77

Green Bean, Mangetout, Babycorn and Pine Nut Stir-fry   78

Okra and Mixed Peppers Jalfrezie   79

Aubergine Caponata   80

Globe Artichoke with Mushroom   82

Stuffed Mediterranean Vegetables   84

Carrot Halwa   85

Carrot Pumpkin Halwa   85

Red, Orange, Yellow & Green
Vegetables

Carrots

Introduction

These brightly coloured members of the plant kingdom contain a wide range of phytochemicals in tasty vegetables like carrots, sweet potatoes, pumpkins, red-orange-yellow and green peppers, butternut squash, aubergine, mushrooms, beetroot, okra, yam, artichoke, asparagus, green beans and broad beans etc.

Fresh Turmeric

The red, orange, yellow colour compounds found in all these vegetables are the powerful fat soluble **antioxidant carotenoids.** There are more than 600 carotenoids; the most widely researched are: alpha carotene, beta carotene, lutein, zeaxanthin, lycopene and beta-cryptoxanthin. About 40 of the naturally occurring carotenoids can be metabolised to vitamin A by the body, but only 3 are most present with respect to total vitamin A intake, and these are alpha carotene, beta carotene and cryptoxanthin.

The most nutritionally significant of these is

beta carotene for it's more present in plant food and hence has higher frequency of consumption, and more research has been done on beta carotene. Carotenoids act as "antioxidants" to neutralise free radicals. Carotenoids help to reduce the risk of various cancers. They enhance the immune function, and decrease the risk of cataracts.

These vegetables are also rich in phenolics, vitamin C and fibre which all help to prevent cancer. For the body to absorb the maximum carotenoids, try to eat all these vegetables slightly cooked, chopped or pureed.

The colourful recipes in this chapter reflect the vibrancy and the natural beauty of the ingredients: starting with fresh juice; butternut soup; the recipes using vegetables like asparagus, green beans and broad beans; colourful aubergine, beetroot; outstanding natural coloured peppers; the stunning globe artichoke and ending with a carrot/pumpkin halwa. I hope your mouth waters as you read through these recipes! Some of the dishes are perfect for lunch, while the rest could be for supper. These recipes are widely loved by my family, friends and students alike.

Coloured Peppers

Carrot, Beetroot, Apple and Turmeric Juice

This is a great morning health tonic experimented by myself over several years. I feel energised for the whole day having taken a large burst of phytonutrients. I take the juice four times a week and for the other three days I either have fresh grapefruit segments or fresh orange juice/or segments.

Carrot juice is a powerful alkalizer, it is often referred to as a miracle juice. Carrot is rich in beta carotene (as the name suggests), an effective antioxidant, which helps to prevent cancer and it also contains fibre which assists in lowering cholesterol.
Apple is a rich source of soluble fibre, pectin.
Beetroot is a potent blood cleanser and is good for the liver.

Turmeric has anti-inflammatory properties which may help to prevent arthritic conditions and latest research suggests that it may reduce Alzheimer's and memory loss as we age.
Fresh turmeric which resembles fresh ginger, is only available from Asian stores, or substitute it with 1 teaspoon of dry turmeric powder for the recipe below.

Ginger is a great option to put into this juice if turmeric is not available, use 2.5cm of ginger. Ginger has anti-inflammatory, anti-parasitic, anti-microbial, anti-ulcer and digestive benefits. It stimulates the circulation and helps prevent nausea. It also helps prevent colon cancer.

This raw juice has alkaline action in the body which helps to dissolve toxic deposits around the joints and other tissues and helps to relieve pain.

Serves 2 - 3

> **2-3 large organic carrots**
> **3 small apples**
> **1 big organic beetroot**
> **5cm piece of fresh turmeric (if available)**
> **or 2.5cm piece of fresh ginger**

Use an electric professional juicer to juice all the vegetables and apples and serve immediately. This recipe makes approximately 500ml of juice.

Beetroot

Squashes

Squashes like butternut, pumpkin, acorn, spaghetti squash, patty pan and gem are amazingly versatile. They can be stuffed, baked, mashed or stir-fried and used in various different recipes.

One of the advantages of **butternut** is that it is available throughout the year. As it cooks, the flesh gets tender and sweet, and the natural butter oozes out of it. The easiest way to cook a butternut is to wash it well and cut it in half lengthways using a big sharp knife. Remove the seeds and the fibre from the cavity and bake for 30-40 minutes until soft and tender. Eat it hot while the butter has melted. Season with a little salt, black pepper and plenty of lime.

For a substantial lunch, stuff the cooked butternut cavity with roasted mixed vegetables, serve it with Tomato & Avocado Raita (page 48).

Another favourite way of using butternut is to make it into a mouth-watering butternut soup, with an oriental twist. As a seasonal alternative, pumpkin could also be used instead of butternut for an equally comforting soup.

Pumpkin contains a rich supply of carotenoids, fibre, potassium, magnesium, vitamin C and vitamin E. It's the synergistic combination of all these health promoting nutrients in pumpkin that makes it special. The high amounts of alpha carotene in pumpkin help to slow the ageing process and give protection against cancer and cataracts.

Butternut Squash,
Pumpkin and Ginger

Butternut Squash, Ginger and Cinnamon Soup

Serves 6 - 8

- 2 tablespoons olive oil
- 1 butternut weighing approximately 450g
- 2 carrots
- 3cm piece fresh ginger
- 850ml water
- 1 teaspoon ground cinnamon powder
- 1 tablespoon dhana jeera; or 1 tablespoon curry powder
- 200ml coconut milk
- seasoning – salt, freshly ground black pepper, lime
- Coriander leaves for garnish

- Peel the butternut, cut it in half length ways, remove the seeds and fibre and dice into cubes.

- Wash the carrots and cut into big chunks

- Peel the ginger and slice finely.

- In a big saucepan, add the olive oil, and sauté the butternut, carrots and ginger together for 5 minutes. Add 850ml water. Bring it to a boil and simmer until the vegetables are soft and cooked.

- Blend the soup to a puree using a hand blender. Add coconut milk, cinnamon powder, dhana jeera/curry powder and season well. Add extra water if necessary to make it into a smooth runny soup. Cook for 10 minutes.

- Serve in a soup bowl, garnish with a few drops of coconut milk, olive oil and a few fresh coriander leaves.

Oven Baked Sweet Potato Chips

Sweet potatoes, the orange flesh variety, are one of the richest sources of beta carotene, a powerful antioxidant which the body converts into vitamin A as needed. It also contains vitamin C, vitamin E, iron, potassium and fibre.

Sweet potatoes are tasty, so easy to cook and are now widely available everywhere, as awareness of their nutritional value increases. I usually substitute a sweet potato for a regular potato, especially in soup recipes.

The oven baked sweet potato chips are crispy on the outside but soft in the middle. They are delicious served hot or cold and are a great healthy option for children to eat and nibble on.

Serves 4

  3 sweet potatoes - peeled
  1-2 tablespoons oil
  1 teaspoon red chilli powder
  salt to taste
  ½ teaspoon freshly ground black pepper
  1 plastic bag

- Pre-heat the oven to 200°C, 400°F, gas mark 6.

- Slice sweet potatoes into finger sized chips.

- In a plastic bag mix the oil, salt, chilli powder and black pepper.

- Put the chips in the bag to coat with the spiced oil.

- When all the chips are coated, empty the chips onto a non-stick baking tray approximately 35cm/28cm and bake in the oven for 20-25 minutes.

* Mixing the sweet potato chips, spices and oil together in a plastic bag is a quick and easy way to coat all the chips. Alternatively, use a big bowl to mix all the ingredients together.

Sweet Potato

Stuffed Mushrooms with a Medley of Coloured Peppers

Mushrooms are the new starfoods – in fact mushrooms like shitake have been used in Japan as immunity boosters. Studies have suggested that substances found in mushrooms have the ability to lower blood cholesterol and mushrooms are also a source of vitamin B, potassium, copper, selenium and lots of other minerals.

Red, yellow and green coloured peppers are rich in antioxidant vitamin C and contain the carotenoids, lutein and zeaxanthin, these two carotenoids are essential for healthy eyes.

Stuffed mushrooms are a well known vegetarian dish which I have made more exciting by adding coriander and chilli-served with the spiced pepper sauce makes them irresistible. Try to use Portobello mushrooms, as the texture and flavour are better.

Serves 4

4 big mushrooms
1 slice of bread – no crust
25g cheese
1 handful coriander
2 garlic cloves
½ long green chilli
12 almonds
4 teaspoons olive oil
salt to taste
freshly ground black pepper
lime juice – a few drops

For the pepper sauce:
1 red pepper – sliced finely
1 yellow pepper – sliced finely
1 green pepper – sliced finely
½ teaspoon red chilli powder
2 tablespoons olive oil
salt to taste
6 tablespoons crème fraiche

- Pre-heat the oven to 200°C, 400°F, Gas Mark 6.

- Remove stalks and arrange the mushrooms in a baking tray.

- Drizzle a teaspoon of olive oil in each mushroom.

- In a food processor, add the mushroom stalks, bread, cheese, coriander, garlic, green chilli and almonds and season well. Mix it all to a fine paste. Fill the mushrooms with this stuffing and bake for 20-25 minutes.

- In the meantime, for the pepper sauce, warm 2 tablespoons oil in a non-stick wok and sauté the sliced mixed peppers for 6-8 minutes. Then stir in the chilli powder, salt and crème fraiche. Serve this spicy sauce with the mushrooms.

Stuffed Portabello Mushrooms
with a Medley of Coloured Peppers

Stir-Fry Quinoa with Peppers

Peppers are rich in vitamin C and contain carotenoids which the body converts to vitamin A as required.

Quinoa looks, cooks and tastes like a cereal but it is actually the dried fruit of a herb which originates in South America. Quinoa is rich in all 8 essential amino acids which makes it a "Complete Protein", ideal for vegetarians. Quinoa is also an excellent source of potassium, iron, a good source of zinc, various B vitamins and fibre.

Sieve it well to get rid of any small grit, then wash and soak for 15 minutes before using. It is essential to soak quinoa to get rid of indigestible saponin, a sticky bitter tasting outer coating of quinoa which protects it while growing - saponin can cause indigestion.

Quinoa flakes are available in health stores and need no cooking. The flakes can be added to cereal for a healthy start to the day.

Uncooked quinoa can be added to soups for a protein boost. Cooked quinoa can be added to salads or use quinoa for a stir-fry as below.

Serves 2 - 3

> **6 tablespoons quinoa**
>
> **2 handfuls of mixed red, yellow and
> green peppers - finely cubed**
>
> **1 tablespoon olive oil**
>
> **light soya sauce - to taste**

- Wash the quinoa and leave to soak for 15 minutes, rinse again and strain through a sieve. To cook, add the soaked quinoa to 600ml of boiling water in a saucepan until the grains open up – approximately 10-15 minutes, be careful not to overcook the quinoa – strain it and let it cool.

- In a wok, warm the oil and stir-fry the mixed peppers. Season well with soya sauce. Add the cooked quinoa, mix well and serve.

  * Serve it as part of a Chinese meal with tofu and vegetables; or it can be eaten hot or cold with a green salad.

Peppers and Quinoa

Broad Beans, Baby Asparagus and Green Beans in Mint Sauce

Use fresh broad beans if in season, the taste is far superior and the time it takes to lovingly open each cooked pod is worth it. Broad beans are rich in folate. When fresh broad beans are not available, soya beans make a good substitute. Asparagus is an excellent diuretic (helps prevent water retention), a source of folate, fibre, vitamin C and potassium. Green beans are good for people with diabetes. The phytonutrients in beans help to enhance insulin efficiency.

This stunning, healthy combination of vegetables can be served hot or cold as a starter on its own or as part of a main meal.

Serves 4

100g broad beans
16 small asparagus spears
100g fine green beans

Dressing:
4 tablespoons good quality olive oil
1 small handful fresh mint leaves
2 teaspoons mint sauce (in bottle)
1 tablespoon vinegar or lime juice
salt, freshly ground black pepper

- Pod the broad beans and cook in boiling water for 3-4 minutes. Skin the beans, to get to the soft green beans (it is tempting to eat the beans warm as they are opened).

- Trim the asparagus and cook in boiling water for 2-3 minutes. Drain and refresh under cold water.

- Trim the green beans and cook in boiling water for 3 minutes or until tender. Drain and refresh under cold running water. Cut into bite size pieces.

- Combine the broad beans, asparagus and green beans in a serving bowl.

- In a separate bowl whisk together the olive oil, mint sauce, mint leaves and vinegar/lime juice.

- Toss the dressing with the vegetable mix and season well.

- * Steam all the above vegetables instead of boiling, for a healthier option.

Broad Beans

Green Bean, Mangetout, Babycorn and Pine Nut Stir-fry

This dish can be served warm as part of a Chinese meal or cold as a side dish with mixed salad leaves. The marriage of the subtle flavours and the crunchy textures makes this quick stir-fry irresistible.

Serves 2 - 4

100g fine green beans	1 teaspoon mustard seeds
100g mange tout (or sugar snap peas)	1 tablespoon pine nuts
50g baby corn	1 tablespoon cashew nuts
2 tablespoons oil	1 tablespoon soya sauce
10 curry leaves (fresh or dry)	salt to taste

- Blanch the green beans in a saucepan of boiling water for 2 minutes. In the same pan add the mangetout and baby corn and blanch for a further 3 minutes.

- Strain the vegetables and refresh in cold water. Trim and cut into bite size pieces.

- In a wok, add 1 tablespoon of oil, sauté the pine nuts and cashew nuts until golden. Remove with a slotted spoon and drain on kitchen paper.

- In the same wok, if required add an extra 1 tablespoon of oil and then add the mustard seeds, curry leaves and cook for one minute. Add the blanched vegetables, mix well, season with salt and soya sauce – cook for 3-4 minutes.

- Remove to a serving plate and garnish with the toasted pine and cashew nuts.

* This dish can also be served with ready bought buckwheat noodles (buckwheat contains all the 8 essential amino acids which makes it an excellent source of protein.)

* If you prefer crunchy vegetables, do not blanch them, instead just trim and cut the raw vegetables into bite size pieces before stir-frying.

Okra and Mixed Peppers Jalfrezie

A lot of people avoid cooking okra because of its stickiness, but they are missing out on a wealth of taste. Stir-frying the okra first in oil removes the stickiness and the addition of a few spices creates a mouthwatering Jalfrezie. This is a colourful curry to serve as part of an Indian meal. The Indian name for okra is bhindi. It is rich in calcium, magnesium, potassium, sodium, and vitamins A and vitamin C.

Serves 3 - 4

225g small delicate okra
half each of red, yellow and
  green peppers – sliced
3 tablespoons oil
1 teaspoon cumin seeds
1 teaspoon salt (or to taste)

1 teaspoon chilli powder
1 tablespoon dhana jeera
a pinch of turmeric
lime juice to taste
handful coriander leaves
natural yogurt - optional

- Wash the okra thoroughly, and top and tail. Wipe each okra with kitchen paper and slice finely lengthways.

- Warm the oil in a wok or a deep frying pan, add the cumin seeds and the sliced okra. Stir gently for 10 minutes, until all the stickiness has gone, add the finely sliced peppers and mix well.

- Add salt, chilli powder, dhana jeera, turmeric, lime juice and stir-fry for a further 5 minutes. Garnish with a few coriander leaves.

- Serve it hot as part of an Indian meal or it makes a delicious cold salad dish when mixed with 8 tablespoons of natural yogurt and served on a bed of lettuce leaves.

Okra

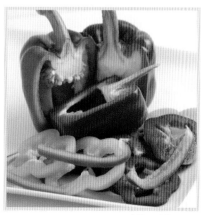

Mixed Peppers

Aubergine Caponata

Aubergine is one of my favourite vegetables and this dish is a great way of enjoying the velvety texture of this versatile vegetable.

The recipe is similar to the traditional Italian dish caponata, originally from Sicily.

The sautéed aubergine caponata can be eaten hot or cold with bread as a starter, or as a dip with some flat-bread, houmous, guacamole, olives, feta cheese or fresh ricotta cheese – an artistic mezze palate of colour and flavour.

Serves 2 - 4

1 long aubergine	salt to taste
2 tablespoons olive oil	freshly ground black pepper
1 tablespoon fennel seeds	1 tablespoon balsamic vinegar
2 tablespoons sultana	1 teaspoon brown sugar
2 tablespoons pine nuts	2 handfuls flat leaf parsley

- Slice the aubergine into very small cubes. Add oil into a non-stick wok and sauté the aubergine until tender, approx 10 minutes.

- Crush the fennel seeds using a rolling pin or a pestle and mortar.

- Add the fennel seeds, sultanas and pine nuts to the aubergine mix and cook for a further 5 minutes. Season with salt, pepper, balsamic vinegar and brown sugar. Garnish with parsley.

* To make aubergine caponata into a pasta sauce, add a good quality home-made tomato sauce (from Penne Arrabiata recipe on page 49).

Aubergine

Globe Artichoke with Mushroom

Fresh globe artichoke is a treat to eat. To prepare an artichoke is a long procedure but once learned, it is easy. Artichoke is rich in compounds called silymarin, which is good for the liver and the base of the succulent leaves are rich in the phytochemical cynarin, which helps to control cholesterol levels.

The recipe below is for two globe artichokes stuffed with mushrooms. Serve it as a starter.

Serves 2

2 large globe artichokes
1 lemon
1 tablespoon olive oil
1 tablespoon butter
225g button mushrooms

1 tablespoon thyme or flat leaf parsley
2 tablespoons crème fraiche
seasoning - salt, pepper, a few drops of Tabasco

- Bring a large saucepan of salted water to the boil. Add a few drops of lemon juice to stop the artichokes browning. To prepare the artichokes, remove the tough outer leaves (about 6-8), cut off the stalks, and with a sharp knife remove one third from the top of each artichoke. Place in the boiling water and cook for half an hour or more, test if it's done by pulling out the first outer leaves, if it comes out easily and is soft and fleshy then it is ready to eat.

- While the artichokes are cooking, prepare the mushroom stuffing. In a wok, melt the butter and olive oil and stir-fry the sliced mushrooms until cooked - between 10-12 minutes. Add the crème fraiche, chopped thyme or parsley and season well.

- Once the artichokes are cooked, remove them from the hot water and drain them upside down. To create a central cavity pull out the small leaves from the middle of each artichoke and with a teaspoon scrape out the fibrous choke. The artichokes with the heart and a few tender leaves on the outside, are now ready for stuffing.

- Just before serving, refresh the artichokes for 2 minutes in hot water. Drain well. Fill the cavity with the warm mushroom mixture and serve. For extra flavour serve a little melted, seasoned butter with lemon juice on the side to dip in the cooked outer leaves. The heart of the artichoke is well worth the wait and the effort in cooking the dish. Good things come to those who wait!

*   The trimmed whole artichoke can be steamed instead of boiling in a saucepan - it takes longer to cook but the flavour is better and it is economical - try and cook 2 or 3 artichokes together in the steamer.

Globe Artichoke

Stuffed Mediterranean Vegetables

This is a timeless classic vegetarian feast. A colourful party dish, ideal for entertaining, as it can be prepared early and cooked later.

Serves 2 - 4

1 aubergine	6 small mushrooms – sliced
1 courgette	1 cup cooked white or brown rice
2 big tomatoes	handful of flat leaf parsley
1 red pepper	handful of coriander
2-4 Portobello mushrooms	1 teaspoon salt
1 tablespoon olive oil	1 teaspoon paprika
	1 teaspoon dried mixed Italian herbs
Stuffing:	1 teaspoon freshly ground black pepper
3 tablespoons olive oil	2 tablespoons pumpkin seeds
1 small onion	2 tablespoons grated cheddar cheese
2 cloves garlic	handful of basil leaves

- Pre-heat the oven to 200°C, 400°F, Gas Mark 6.
- Wash and cut the aubergine in half lengthways. Hollow out the centre using a sharp knife and a teaspoon. Cut the aubergine flesh into small pieces – to be used as the stuffing. Prepare the courgette in the same way, and use the courgette flesh for the stuffing.
- Blanch the aubergine and courgette shells in boiling water for 2 minutes. Drain well.
- Slice the tops off the tomatoes and use as lids for the tomato cases. Scoop out the inside of the tomato cases using a teaspoon.
- Slice the pepper in half and remove the seeds and core. Trim the stalks of the Portabello mushrooms – use them for the stuffing. Place all the prepared vegetables in a big baking dish and drizzle a little olive oil over the inside of the vegetable cases.
- **For the stuffing:** In a saucepan, stir-fry the onion and garlic in 3 tablespoons of olive oil for a few minutes. Add the finely chopped aubergines, courgettes, mushrooms and tomatoes. Cook for 5 more minutes. Add the cooked rice, parsley, coriander, salt, paprika, mixed herbs and black pepper. Cook for a further 5 minutes. Mix the stuffing thoroughly and spoon it into the prepared vegetable cases. Sprinkle some pumpkin seeds in all the cases. Bake, covered with aluminium foil, for 20 minutes. Remove the foil, add the grated cheese on top and bake for a further 20 minutes until it is thoroughly cooked.
- **Serve garnished with basil leaves.** To accompany the stuffed vegetables, serve with the tomato sauce from the Penne Arrabiata recipe on page 49.
- * As an alternative, instead of rice, use cooked quinoa or cooked couscous for stuffing the vegetables.

Carrot Halwa

Carrot halwa is a traditional Indian dessert, popular for festive occasions and wedding meals, usually served hot with vanilla ice-cream or cold with single cream. It keeps in the fridge for 4-5 days and freezes well.

Serves 6 - 8

450g carrots, peeled

1 tablespoon ghee or butter

a handful of whole skinned almonds, pistachio nuts and cashew nuts

1 teaspoon cardamon powder

300ml milk

100g sugar

1 teaspoon rosewater (optional)

6-8 saffron strands

- Shred the carrots finely in a food processor or use a hand grater.

- In a large saucepan, melt the ghee or butter and add the almonds, pistachios, and cashew nuts. Stir for 1 minute.

- Add the shredded carrots and stir-fry for 10 minutes over a medium heat, until the carrots have softened and cooked. Add the milk and cook for 10 more minutes, stirring 2-3 times.

- Add the sugar and cook for a further 10 minutes, making sure that the mixture does not stick to the saucepan. Mix everything very well. The halwa should now be ready – thick and glossy. Add the rosewater, cardamon powder and saffron for fragrance and serve hot or cold.

Carrot Pumpkin Halwa

Alternatively you can cook a very tasty halwa by adding pumpkin. Use 250g of carrots and 250g of pumpkin and follow the recipe as above. Asian and Caribbean stores sell large pumpkins, cut into sections, which would be ideal to use in this recipe.

Chapter 6

Introduction   88

Fresh Mango Juice with Ginger   89

Apple and Cranberry Spritzer   89

Watermelon Granita   89

Mango Lassi   89

Dry Fruit Compote   90

Cinnamon Poached Pears   91

Avocado Fool with Pistachio Nuts   92

Pomegranate with Yogurt Shrikand   95

Rainbow Coloured Fruits

Mixed Fruits

Introduction

Blueberries, strawberries, cranberries, raspberries, pomegranates, grapes, apples, apricots, prunes, peaches, kiwis, cantaloupe melons, watermelons, papaya, mangoes, oranges, tangerines, red grapefruit and many more exotic fruits, have a wide range of phytochemicals, which help to decrease the risk of heart disease, cancer and help to boost the immune system.

Citrus fruits have been called "a total anti-cancer package" for they have a high concentration of **flavonoids** and **vitamin C,** which all act as powerful antioxidants – and protect cells from damage caused by free radicals. The flavonoids are effective in lowering blood lipids like cholesterol and triglycerides. Vitamin C helps to return the antioxidant vitamin E to its active form and also helps to prevent cataracts in the eyes which are often formed by free radical damage to the lenses.

The **soluble fibre** of the fruits, especially pectin, helps to protect against cardiovascular disease. Try to eat segments of grapefruit and citrus fruits instead of just juice, for most of the fibre, pectin, is in the membrane and juice sacs of the fruit. The **pectin,** especially in apples, helps to stabilise blood sugar by delaying the absorption of sugar in the intestine, a great help for anyone with type 2 diabetes.

Prunes and blueberries are on top of the list of fruits on the **ORAC score,** in which foods are ranked according to their oxygen radical absorption capacity, or how well they act as antioxidants. The flavonoid anthocyanin, which gives blueberries their intense blue colour is a powerful antioxidant, it has anti-inflammatory properties. Blueberries are often called "brain berries" and "youth berries" for their anti-ageing properties - "forever young!".

Cranberries and blueberries can help prevent urinary tract infections, for example cystitis, for a naturally occurring substance in these berries prevents the bacteria that causes cystitis from sticking to the walls of the urethra.

Cherries, strawberries, grapes and raspberries all contain antioxidant **phenolics** like ellagic acids, which may help to deactivate carcinogens that lead to cancerous growths.

Despite all the recipes I prefer to eat my fruits uncooked, unaltered, whole and as natural and as fresh as possible, ideally with a two hour gap between meals. Fruits are the perfect energy booster. Sometimes a dessert is needed, so I have recipes for Dry Fruit Compote, Pomegranate with Yogurt Shrikand, Avocado Fool and Poached Pears which can all be served with any cuisine.

Mango

Fresh Mango Juice with Ginger

When fresh ripe mangoes are available, the best drink to accompany a spicy meal is mango juice – spark it up with ginger powder.

Serves 2 - 4

4 ripe mangoes
1 teaspoon ginger powder (optional)
1-2 tablespoons sugar

- Skin the mangoes and scoop out the flesh. Mix with water (the quantity depending on the consistency of juice you prefer) and sugar to taste.

- Blend in a liquidiser until smooth, cover the juice and chill it. Serve in glass bowls, for extra bite, sprinkle some ground ginger on top.

Spirit Lifting Cocktails without the "Spirits"
Apple and Cranberry Spritzer

In a jug mix two parts of apple juice, one part of cranberry juice, and one finely cubed fresh apple. Top up with lemonade, crushed ice and serve chilled. Add a few fresh mint leaves as decoration.

Watermelon Granita

Watermelon is an excellent source of vitamin C and the antioxidant carotenoid lycopene.

Use a food processor to purée the watermelon with some seeds, keep it chunky. Sweeten it with sugar if necessary. Freeze it for one hour or less. Stir vigorously with a fork. Serve it in cocktail glasses with finely chopped mint. It has the consistency of a granita.

Mango Lassi

Mango is an excellent source of beta carotene (the body converts it to vitamin A as needed), vitamin C, potassium and fibre.

Lassi is a popular drink made from equal quantities of natural yoghurt and water – mixed with a whisk or a hand blender.

To prepare the delicious mango lassi, use an electric hand blender and mix together equal quantities of natural yoghurt, water, and fresh ripe mango or tinned mango juice. Add sugar to taste and mix well, until it is all frothy on top. Serve in tall glasses with crushed ice.

Dry Fruit Compote

Dry apricots are rich in beta-carotene (the body converts it into vitamin A as needed), potassium, boron and fibre.

Prunes are listed very high on the ORAC score - which is a measure of the foods antioxidant value. Prunes contain beta-carotene, boron and copper.

Try to use dry apricots and prunes without the preservative sulphur dioxide as this can trigger asthma attacks. If they are not available, rinse the apricots and prunes well with warm water before using them for this recipe.

Almonds are one of the best sources of vitamin E, a potent antioxidant and they also provide protein and calcium.

The zest of orange contains limone, a citrus oil, which is a chemo-preventive phyto-nutrient and it can help to lower levels of harmful LDL (low density lipoprotein) cholesterol.

Serves 4

10 dry apricots
10 dry prunes
30 almonds - skinned
juice of 2 fresh oranges - 200ml
1 tablespoon grated zest of orange

2 teaspoons lime juice
2-3 tablespoons honey
cream or yoghurt

- To skin the almonds put them in boiling water for 2/3 minutes, drain the almonds and the skin will slip off easily.

- In a glass bowl, mix together orange juice, orange zest, lime juice and honey to taste.

- Add the apricots, prunes and skinned almonds to the syrup. Let them soak for a few hours.

- Serve this tasty, colourful and healthy mixture for breakfast on its own or with cream/yoghurt as a dessert.

Cinnamon Poached Pears

The fusion of the traditional poached pear dessert and the cinnamon spices makes this classic dish extremely appealing and healthy.

Research studies suggest that the spice cinnamon is of great benefit to people who suffer with type 2 diabetes.

Serves 6

6 small slightly ripe pears
600ml water
75g light brown sugar
4-5 cinnamon sticks

juice of half a lemon
cinnamon powder
single cream or ice-cream (optional)

- Wash and gently peel the pears, keeping the stalks intact.

- In a saucepan, add the water, sugar, cinnamon sticks and lemon juice.

- Bring the water to a boil and add the pears. Lower the temperature, cover the saucepan and simmer for 25-30 minutes, until the pears are soft. The syrup should reduce to about half of the original quantity.

- Place the pears and the syrup in a serving bowl, and chill them until they are ready to be served.

- Sprinkle cinnamon powder on the pears and serve with single cream or ice cream.

Avocado Fool with Pistachio Nuts

My passion for avocado is reflected in this light, tropical fruit fool, which is my own invention. The pale green colour of avocado and pistachio nuts, topped with kiwi and passion fruit, is most refreshing after a hot, spicy meal.

Avocado contains monounsaturated fat (which is good for the heart), iron, copper, potassium, folate, vitamin B, vitamin K and vitamin E. It is easily digested and contains the potent antioxidant glutathione, which helps to de-activate free radicals.

Banana is packed with potassium which helps to lower blood pressure.

Pineapple contains the enzyme bromelin which prevents bruising and it also has powerful anti-inflammatory properties.

Kiwi fruit is rich in vitamin C, while passion fruit contains potassium.

Pistachio nuts contain co-enzyme Co-Q10, vitamin B, vitamin E, iron, zinc, potassium and fibre.

All the above phytonutrients are essential to boost the immune system.

Serves 4 - 6

2 big ripe avocados - skinned and stoned	a little sugar to taste
½ banana	75g whole pistachio nuts
4 slices fresh or tinned pineapple	2 sliced kiwi fruits
175ml single cream	2 passion fruits - seeds

- Put the avocado, banana, pineapple, cream and sugar in a blender or a food processor and blend to a smooth purée. Remove to a serving bowl, add the pistachio nuts and mix well.

- Decorate with passion fruit seeds and slices of kiwi fruit on top. Cover with cling film and chill well. Try to prepare this dessert no more than 1- 2 hours before the meal in order to prevent the avocado from discolouring. You can, of course, serve it straight away if you have used chilled ingredients.

Pomegranate

Pomegranate with Yogurt Shrikand

Shrikand is an Indian sweet made with natural yogurt and nuts. By adding pomegranate it can be turned into a great festive dish.

Silky-soft, cold shrikand, flavoured with saffron, makes the perfect end to a meal on a hot summer's day. You can make it early, as shrikand can be kept in the fridge for a few days.

The probiotics (good bacteria) present in yogurt help to digest the food and strengthen the immune system. Yogurt is also a good source of calcium.

The recent craze for pomegranate is due to all its anti-ageing properties, the little red ruby seeds will be the jewel of my dessert!

Serves 2 - 3

425g natural bio-live yogurt	6-8 saffron strands
2 tablespoons sugar	1 handful pistachio nuts
½ teaspoon ground cardamon	1 whole pomegranate seeds

- Separate the whey from the yogurt using the quick method described below.

- The traditional method of separating the whey from the yogurt is to tie the yogurt in a cheese cloth and hang it for 3-4 hours. However, a much quicker and easier method is to place a few layers of newspaper on a table, put a clean muslin or a tea towel on top, place the yogurt on half the tea towel and fold the other half on top. Cover with several more layers of newspaper and place a weight on top. This is a sandwich of newspaper, tea towel, yogurt, tea towel, newspaper. The whey will separate very quickly and will be absorbed by the newspaper.

- 425g yogurt takes less than 20 minutes to separate and will produce about 4 tablespoons of yogurt solids.

- Put the yogurt solids, sugar and cardamon in a bowl and mix well for a few minutes, to get a smooth shrikand. (Always use 2 parts yogurt solids to 1 part sugar). Spread the saffron strands on top, cover and refrigerate until ready to eat. The saffron will slowly seep through the shrikand giving a beautiful colour and fragrance.

- Decorate with pistachio nuts and the pomegranate seeds before serving.

Pomegranate with
Yogurt Shrikand

Chapter 7

Introduction	98
Chickpea and Yogurt Soup with Guacamole	99
Tuscan White Bean Soup with Rosemary	100
Puy Lentils with Herb Chutney	101
Spiced Sprouting Bean Salad	102
Buckwheat, Hazelnut and Three Bean Salad	103
Pea, Mint, Feta Cheese Salad with Roasted Butternut Squash, Red Peppers, Pumpkin Seeds and Quinoa	104
Black-eye Bean Curry	105
Houmous - Avocado Houmous - Roasted Red Pepper Houmous	107
Falafel	108
Moroccan Style Green Lentils	109

Beans, Peas & Lentils

Black-eye Beans

Introduction

This group is known as pulses and, as the name suggests, are really the **heart** of a vegetarian diet. The popular and widely available pulses are chick peas, black-eye beans, kidney beans, moong beans, cannellini beans, soya beans, aduki beans, dry peas and lentils. All pulses are a great source of protein, carbohydrates, vitamins, minerals and fibre. Pulses contain **soluble and insoluble fibre.** This high fibre content helps to reduce blood lipid levels, especially LDL, low density lipoprotein (the bad cholesterol), and it also helps to control diabetes by slowing the amount and pace of sugar entering the blood stream.

Beans, especially black-eye beans, contain a high amount of **folate**, a B vitamin, which helps to regulate blood levels of homocysteine, a naturally occurring amino acid in the body. At increased levels homocysteine can become toxic and contribute to the development of atherosclerosis and heart disease. Beans also contain liganins and isoflavones which may have a chemo-preventive effect on hormone related cancers. It has been often quoted that nature couldn't have invented a more perfect food than beans.

Bean protein lacks two amino acids (with the exception of soya beans which contain all the essential amino acids) so to make up for this, always serve other protein rich foods during the day. For example, most international cuisines combine a grain with a bean, like rice and dal, couscous and chickpeas, tacos and kidney beans, beans on toast.

The importance of soya beans has been allocated a separate chapter page 55….

Being born into a vegetarian family, cooking with pulses comes naturally to me. I love to eat beans, peas and lentils at every main meal and I hope these recipes inspire you to start cooking with pulses and add a new variation and dimension to vegetarian food.

Houmous

Chickpea and Yogurt Soup with Guacamole

Chickpeas contain protein, fibre and folate which helps to protect against heart disease, and phytoestrogen isoflavones which may help to delay and prevent hormone related cancer. I love this unique soup for all the healthy ingredients it contains.

Serves 4 - 5

410g tin chickpeas
2 tablespoons olive oil
225ml natural yogurt (half big carton)
600ml water
2 tablespoons gram flour or corn flour
1 teaspoon caraway seeds
1 teaspoon cumin seeds
1 bunch spring onions
½ bunch fresh mint
3 tablespoons tahini paste
1 lime – zest

salt to taste
freshly ground black pepper

For guacamole:
1 avocado
2 handfuls coriander leaves
½ green chilli - chopped
1 teaspoon lime juice
½ teaspoon salt

- Prepare a yogurt lassi by mixing yogurt, water and gram flour (or corn flour) in a jug. Blend well using an electric hand blender.

- In a saucepan, add the olive oil, caraway seeds, cumin seeds, and sauté the chopped spring onion for 3-4 minutes. Pour the yogurt lassi into the saucepan and bring to a boil.

- Drain the tin of chickpeas and rinse well under cold water. Reserve 2 tablespoons of chickpeas and a few mint leaves for garnish. Add the remaining chickpeas, mint leaves and lime zest to the yogurt mixture in the saucepan.

- Add tahini paste and season well with salt and pepper, and cook uncovered for 10 minutes. Cool the mixture a little and then blend to a smooth soup puree (add extra water to thin the soup if necessary). For a finer and silkier soup you can sieve the soup.

- For the guacamole mix avocado flesh, coriander, chilli, lime juice and salt with a fork to make a thick chunky guacamole.

To serve:
In a soup bowl, add a few whole chickpeas, pour in some hot soup and add a tablespoon of guacamole on top. Garnish with mint leaves. This refreshing and filling soup can be served luke warm on a hot summer's day.

Tuscan White Bean Soup with Rosemary

A healthy option for this delicious soup, if you have a juicer, is to make your own vegetable stock by juicing 1 whole celery, 6 medium carrots and a handful of parsley. Alternatively use stock powder.

Serves 6 - 8

850ml vegetable stock
2 tablespoons olive oil (plus extra oil for garnish)
1 teaspoon caraway seeds
4 bay leaves
1 big shallot or onion
1 small carrot – cut in small matchsticks
few French green beans (approx 12)
410g tin cannellini beans – drained and rinsed
salt, freshly ground black pepper
1 tablespoon rosemary (fresh)

- Prepare a good fresh vegetable stock by juicing 1 whole celery, 6 carrots and ½ bunch flat-leaf parsley. Add extra water to make it up to 850ml. Alternatively use 1 tablespoon of Marigold stock powder to 850ml of water.

- In a big saucepan, add 2 tablespoons of olive oil, caraway seeds and bay leaves, and sauté the chopped shallot or onion for 5 minutes.

- Add the vegetable stock, carrots, French green beans – trimmed and cut in 5cm pieces, and the cannellini beans.

- Season well with salt, pepper and lots of fresh rosemary.

- Cook for 20 minutes.

Serve drizzled with extra olive oil and warm Italian bread.

* Instead of a can of cannellini beans, use 125g dry white cannellini beans. Soak the beans for 8 hours and cook in a big saucepan until soft to touch (approx 1 hour). Use the liquid that the beans have been cooked in as part of the stock.

Puy Lentils with Herb Chutney

These dark green small lentils, grown in the region of Le Puy en Velay in France, have a strong earthy aroma, with a very sweet and nutty flavour. They need no pre-soaking and can be served hot or cold with lots of recipes. It is my firm favourite lentil, tasty and so quick to prepare, yet full of goodness.

Use Puy lentils instead of the green lentils in the *Moroccan Style Green Lentils* dish (page 109).

Serves 4

125g Puy lentils – rinsed	*Herb chutney:*
1 red pepper	1 bunch coriander
2 tablespoons olive oil	1 green chilli - chopped
salt	1 teaspoon fresh ginger
freshly ground black pepper	½ bunch mint
	½ bunch flat leaf parsley
	2 teaspoons lime juice
	½ teaspoon salt

- Pre-heat the oven to 200°C, 400°F, gas mark 6.

- Cut the red pepper in half, de-seed and roast in a hot oven for 20 minutes. Transfer it to a small plate and cover with cling film. When cold the skin of the pepper peels off easily - chop it into bite size pieces.

- Cook the lentils in 600ml of water for 12-15 minutes, until the lentils are cooked but firm to the bite. Do not overcook the lentils. Strain and empty into a large glass bowl.

- Add the olive oil to the warm cooked lentils and season to taste.

- To prepare the herb chutney put all the ingredients in a blender and whiz to a smooth paste.

- Add the chopped cooked red pepper and the herb chutney to the lentils, mix well and leave it covered for ½ hour before serving for all the flavours to combine.

- Serve on a bed of green mixed lettuce leaves or as part of a summer feast.

Spiced Sprouting Bean Salad

Packets of sprouting bean salad – a mixture of chickpeas, aduki beans, moong beans and lentil sprouts – are now available in many supermarkets and health food stores. This recipe is based on the bought mixture but, if you prefer, you can use any combination of bean sprouts or even sprout your own!

It is also easy to sprout fenugreek seeds – wash the seeds well, soak for a little while in warm water and they sprout in 2 days. Fenugreek sprouts are delicious in taste.

Sprouted beans are nutritious. Serve this lightly spiced salad as a starter, or as a side dish with any selection of curries and rice.

Serves 2

1 tablespoon oil
½ teaspoon mustard seeds
1 teaspoon cumin seeds
1 teaspoon grated fresh ginger
1 green chilli - de-seeded and
  finely chopped
150g sprouted beans

1 teaspoon salt (or less)
½ teaspoon chilli powder
1 teaspoon lime juice
2-3 tablespoons yogurt
a few chicory leaves (red or white leaves)

• Warm the oil in a wok or a deep frying pan and add the mustard and cumin seeds. When the mustard seeds pop, mix in the ginger, green chilli and sprouted beans.

• Add the salt and chilli powder and flavour with lime juice. Stir-fry for 5-8 minutes.

• When cold (after about 10 minutes), mix the bean salad with the yogurt or serve the yogurt separately, and garnish with the chicory leaves.

Spiced Sprouting Bean Salad

Buckwheat, Hazelnut and Three Bean Salad

Buckwheat is the fruit of a plant which is related to rhubarb. It is safe for people who suffer from wheat allergies as it is not actually a kind of wheat. It is rich in fibre and is also a good source of protein, especially the essential amino acid, lysine. Buckwheat has a high concentration of the flavonoid rutin, which helps to strengthen blood vessels and is useful for anyone who bruises easily. Buckwheat is available from major supermarkets.

Hazelnuts are rich in vitamin E, manganese and zinc.

Serves 4 - 6

100g buckwheat
400g tin mixed three beans
2 handfuls hazelnuts
½ bunch coriander
salt to taste

Dressing:
2 tablespoons olive oil
1 tablespoon balsamic vinegar
1 tablespoon mint sauce
2 teaspoons honey
1 teaspoon French mustard
2 teaspoons lime juice

- Heat 200ml water in a saucepan. Wash the buckwheat thoroughly and add to the boiling water. Reduce the heat, simmer for 6 minutes or till the buckwheat is cooked – strain and let it cool.

- Rinse the beans under cold running water and mix in with the cooked buckwheat.

- Chop the coriander finely in a food processor.

- Lightly dry roast the hazelnuts in a non-stick frying pan or in a hot oven.

- Mix all the ingredients for the dressing in a jar (olive oil, balsamic vinegar, mint sauce, honey, mustard and lime juice) and season well.

- To serve, combine the buckwheat, beans, coriander, hazelnuts and the dressing together in a salad bowl and let it marinate before serving.

Pea, Mint, Feta Cheese Salad with Roasted Butternut Squash, Red Peppers, Pumpkin Seeds and Quinoa

This exotic salad is an exciting way to obtain the maximum phytonutrients from tasty ingredients – in one meal. Its simple to put together, can be eaten for two days and is an ideal packed lunch to take to work.

Serves 4 - 6

4 tablespoons peas (fresh)	*Dressing:*
½ bunch mint leaves	2 tablespoons olive oil
100g feta cheese	1 tablespoon red wine vinegar
1 butternut squash	or lime juice
2 red peppers	1 teaspoon honey
2 handfuls pumpkin seeds	salt to taste
4 tablespoons quinoa	

- Pre-heat the oven to 220°C, 400°F, Gas Mark 6.

- Blanch fresh peas in boiling water for 4 minutes (or steam), drain and cool.

- Peel and cube a medium sized butternut squash. Roast it in a baking dish for about 25 minutes, turning half way through, until the squash is soft and cooked.

- Cut the red peppers in four slices and roast in another baking dish at the same time for 20 minutes. When cold, remove the skin and slice into small cubes.

- Roast pumkin seeds for 5 minutes till lightly browned.

- Wash the quinoa and soak it for 20 minutes. Cook the quinoa in 600ml of water until the grains open (approximately 10-12 minutes), strain it and let it cool.

- Combine all the dressing ingredients in a jar - shake it well.

- To assemble the salad, mix the peas, mint leaves, butternut squash, red peppers, pumpkin seeds and quinoa in a salad bowl. Pour on the dressing as required. Crumble over the feta cheese and enjoy it.

  * As an alternative, use buckwheat or couscous instead of quinoa.
  * Soya beans can be used instead of fresh peas.
  * Sweet potato - easy to peel and cube, can be used instead of butternut squash.

Black-eye Bean Curry

Black-eye Beans

Black-eye beans rank as the highest source of **folate**, even higher than spinach, cabbage and Swiss chard. The folate is a B vitamin found in common plant foods, it is used in the body to manufacture amino acids and is also used in the production of DNA. It works with vitamin B12 to support the growth of rapidly dividing cells and it is excellent for heart health. Folate deficiency has been found to lead to anaemia, weakness and depression.

Dry black-eye beans are widely available and easy to use as they only require a good soaking in warm water before cooking, for approximately 40 minutes. Cooked beans can be added to salad or lightly cooked in olive oil, with garlic and herbs to serve as a side dish. Tinned black-eye beans are very handy to use and are available from most supermarkets – add a range of Indian spices and transform them into a very tasty and satisfying curry, ready to eat in a short time. Serve the curry as part of an Indian meal with rice and naan bread.

Serves 4

400g tin black-eye beans	1 teaspoon salt (or less to taste)
2 tablespoons oil	1 teaspoon chilli powder
$\frac{1}{2}$ teaspoon mustard seeds	$\frac{1}{4}$ teaspoon ground turmeric
$\frac{1}{2}$ teaspoon cumin seeds	1 tablespoon dhana jeera
$\frac{1}{2}$ teaspoon asafoetida	$\frac{1}{2}$ teaspoon garam masala
1 teaspoon grated fresh ginger	1 teaspoon lime juice
1 tablespoon gram flour	1 tablespoon chopped spring onions
$\frac{1}{2}$ green pepper, cut into cubes	
3-4 tomatoes – skinned and chopped	
or 3 tablespoons tinned tomatoes	

- Open the tin of black-eye beans and rinse the beans in cold water to get rid of the thick liquid that sticks to them.

- Heat the oil in a pan over medium heat. Add the mustard seeds, wait till the mustard seeds start popping and add cumin seeds, asafoetida, ginger and gram flour. Stir it for 2 minutes, then add the green pepper, tomatoes, salt, chilli powder, turmeric, dhana jeera and garam masala, one by one. Cook for 3 minutes.

- Add the black-eye beans and 175ml water to the pan, mix well, cover and simmer for 10 minutes.

- Add the lime juice and garnish with the spring onions before serving.

Houmous

This is my version of the traditional Middle Eastern dish using chickpeas. I think houmous is a **perfect dish** full of phytonutrients. It only takes a few minutes to prepare such a tasty healthy dip. The chickpeas contain protein, fibre and folate which help to protect against heart disease, and phytoestrogen isoflavones which might help to delay hormone related cancers.

Garlic is anti-bacterial and anti-viral. It strengthens the heart and helps to boost the immune system.

Tahini is a sesame seed paste which contains a lot of calcium, fibre and vitamin E. Yogurt contains probiotic bacteria which helps to digest the food and improve the immune system. Lime contains vitamin C – an antioxidant.

Combine the whole lot with good quality extra virgin olive oil which has perfect monounsaturated fat - good for the heart. Home-made houmous is easy, economical and you can control the amount of oil and salt that you use. In fact, you can also make an oil free houmous by not adding any olive oil to the mixture – it tastes just as good!

Make 3 different varieties of houmous, using this basic recipe.
Serve it with crudités of celery, radish, carrots and red peppers or with grilled pitta bread.

410g tin chick peas (organic if available)	1-2 tablespoons olive oil
3 tablespoons natural yogurt	salt to taste
3 tablespoons tahini (sesame seed paste)	lime juice to taste
2 garlic cloves – optional	½ teaspoon paprika

- Rinse the chickpeas well and put in a blender, reserving a few chickpeas for garnish. Add 1 tablespoon of olive oil, yogurt, tahini and garlic, and season well with salt and lime juice. Blend it to a smooth paste by adding 1-2 tablespoons of water as required. For an extra smooth houmous use a liquidiser to mix all the ingredients.

- Remove to a serving bowl. Garnish with the remaining chickpeas, olive oil and paprika. Chill well for all the flavours to mingle.

* **Avocado Houmous** – add a small avocado to the above recipe it makes an extra healthy version, lime green in colour and sweeter to taste.

* **Roasted Red Pepper Houmous** – the addition of a roasted red pepper (use grilled roast peppers from a jar or roast your own) creates a pink houmous.

Houmous with celery, radish and carrot

Falafel

This Egyptian style falafel uses dry broad beans and a few chickpeas, giving a much softer texture and sweeter taste to the falafel.

Approx 25 Falafel

100g split dry broad beans
50g dry chick peas
1 teaspoon cumin seeds
salt to taste
2 handfuls fresh flat leaf parsley
2 handfuls fresh coriander

1 green long chilli
1 garlic clove (optional)
½ teaspoon soda bicarbonate
   (or baking powder)
linseeds or sesame seeds for decoration
oil for frying

- Soak the dry chickpeas overnight.

- Soak the split dry broad beans for 4 hours.

- Drain the pulses and grind the chickpeas and broad beans together to a coarse paste in a blender with cumin seeds, salt to taste, parsley, coriander, chilli and garlic, if using – and add a little water if needed. Chill the mixture.

- Add ½ teaspoon soda bicarbonate to the mixture when ready to cook, mix well and make small balls of the mixture or use a falafel disk to form equal size balls. Decorate with a few linseeds or sesame seeds.

- Deep fry and serve with flat pitta bread, houmous (page 107), tahini dip (page 127) and bulgar wheat salad (page 115).

* Alternatively for an even healthier version, instead of deep frying, steam the falafel. When cold, sauté in a frying pan with a little oil.

* If split dry broad beans are not available, soak whole dry broad beans for 4 hours and remove as much of the husk as possible before grinding the beans.

Moroccan Style Green Lentils

Green lentils, widely available in all supermarkets, need no pre-soaking and cook in 15-20 minutes. Ready made Harissa paste is a strong chilli paste, made with dry red chillies, aromatic spices and oil. It is available in bottles or small tubes – freeze the extra Harissa paste for further use.

You can even substitute Puy lentils for the green lentils as an alternative for this dish.

Serves 6

225g green lentils	2 garlic cloves - chopped
2 tablespoons olive oil	2 teaspoon cumin seeds
2 bay leaves	1 teaspoon salt
1 cinnamon stick	1 teaspoon cinnamon powder
1 dry red chilli	1 teaspoon cumin powder
1 small red onion - sliced	1 teaspoon Harissa paste – or less

- Cook the green lentils in water for 15 minutes until slightly soft to touch, drain and reserve.

- In another saucepan, add the olive oil, bay leaves, cinnamon stick, dry red chilli, and cumin seeds and sauté the sliced red onion for 4 minutes. Add the garlic and stir-fry.

- Add the cooked lentils and the remaining spices to taste, plus 300ml water. Simmer for 20 minutes, until the liquid is reduced.

- Serve with pitta bread or boiled rice.

Chapter 8

Introduction   112

Barley and Red Lentil Broth   113

Bulgar Wheat Salad with Coriander, Parsley,
Mint and Walnut   115

Polenta and Mushroom Stir-fry   116

Saffron Rice   117

Baked Sweetcorn with Asparagus   119

Spiced Oats   120

Naan Bread   121

Grains

Basmati Rice

Introduction

The basic staple ingredient of every world cuisine, such as Indian, Chinese, African European, Italian, American or Mexican food, is **grains.** The well known grains are wheat, corn, rice, oats, barley, bulgar wheat, couscous, millet, rye and spelt.

Whole grains (with bran, endosperm and germ in tact) are a good source of fibre, especially the soluble **fibre** found in oats, which helps to provide protection against heart disease, obesity and help control diabetes. Whole grains contain vitamin E, an antioxidant which protects body cells from oxidative damage caused by free radicals; they also contain B vitamins and are a great source of protein. Grains also contain phenolic acid which is a strong antioxidant, and which may help to protect the body's DNA from carcinogens.

Wheatgerm is full of nutrients, it is widely available from most health stores and supermarkets. Wheatgerm is a plant source of omega 3 fatty acid which helps thin the blood, lower blood pressure and has anti-inflammatory properties – just 2 tablespoons of wheatgerm sprinkled on yogurt or cereal is enough to get a daily boost of this essential omega 3 fatty acid.

I have tried to include recipes for most of the popular grains. The recipes reflect my love for international vegetarian cuisine, Indian, Continental, Middle Eastern and Chinese. This is my way of getting a balance of most phytonutrients and as the saying goes "variety is the spice of life".

Other popular grains which are full of nutrients that I have not included in my recipes but would like to highlight are spelt and millet.

Spelt is a variety of wheat, used in ancient times, which is coming back into fashion because it is rich in protein and iron. Pasta made from spelt is available from some supermarkets and can be used instead of normal pasta, the flavour is earthy and sweet.

Millet is a popular grain used in India, millet flour is used in making the Indian bread – rotla. Millet contains protein, iron and silica and is gluten free – a great alternative to wheat.

Barley and Red Lentil Broth

Barley is the oldest cultivated cereal, with amazing nutritional and health properties. Barley contains calcium, potassium and vitamin B – it is excellent for anyone recovering from illness or stress.

This soup was introduced by Jenifer Courtney who was born and raised in Belfast and suggests eating it with Irish wheaten bread. It is the ultimate comfort food if you are feeling under the weather.

Serves 4 - 6

3 litres vegetable stock
1 ½ handfuls split red lentils
1 handful dried peas
½ handful barley
1 large carrot
1 large leek
2 celery sticks
handful flat leaf parsley
chilli oil for garnish (optional)

- Boil the vegetable stock in a big saucepan. (Prepare a good vegetable stock at home or alternatively use 1-2 tablespoons of Marigold vegetable stock and 3 litres of water).

- Add the red lentils, dried peas and barley. Cook for 15 minutes and then add the chopped carrot, leek and celery. Simmer for 45 minutes to an hour.

- Serve garnished with parsley and chilli oil (optional).

* Some supermarkets sell ready mixed soup and broth mix. If available, use 3 tablespoons of this mix for the above recipe instead of the red lentils, dried peas and barley. Use the same quantity of vegetables as above.

Bulgar Wheat Salad with Coriander, Parsley, Mint and Walnuts

Bulgar wheat used in Middle Eastern cooking, in dishes such as tabouleh, is wheat that is parboiled, dried and cracked. It's available in most supermarkets. It is an excellent source of fibre, contains potassium, vitamin B, and has some iron and calcium. This is one of my favourite salads. I love the combination of this recipes's ingredients, parsley, coriander, mint, tomatoes, walnuts and olive oil, all full of phytonutrients. I eat it often and it is a perfect dish to take to a friend's house to share.

Serves 4 - 6

100g bulgar wheat
600ml water
4 handfuls flat leaf parsley – chopped
4 handfuls coriander – chopped
2 handfuls fresh mint – chopped
10 cherry tomatoes - cut in half
1 bunch spring onion – chopped

Dressing:
juice of 1-2 limes
4 tablespoons olive oil
rock salt to taste
2 tablespoons chopped walnuts

- Cook the bulgar wheat according to the instructions on the packet – in boiling water for 15 minutes until tender. Strain the bulgar wheat and transfer it to a serving bowl.

- When the cooked bulgar wheat is cold, add in the finely chopped parsley, coriander, fresh mint, tomatoes, spring onion and walnuts.

- Add the olive oil, lime juice and salt to taste. Keep the salad in the fridge and allow all the flavours to blend before serving.

Polenta and Mushroom Stir-fry

Polenta, used in Italian cooking, is white or yellow corn flour – it is available in most supermarkets. To cook polenta, follow the instructions on the packet or cook using my method where polenta is first stir-fried in oil and cooked in the liquid afterwards – both methods work well. I still remember the flavours of a memorable lunch served in Venice - it was grilled polenta, with fresh tomato sauce and a big grilled tomato with lots of fresh basil - so simple, yet so stunning.

Serves 2

100ml milk

300ml water

1 tablespoon olive oil

100g polenta

pinch of salt

2 tablespoons grated cheese
    (parmesan or cheddar)

For the mushroom stir-fry:

225g mushrooms – sliced

1 tablespoon olive oil

2 teaspoons butter

1 teaspoon caraway seeds

salt to taste

parsley or basil to garnish

cheese for garnish

4 tablespoons tomato sauce
    (page 49) (optional)

For the polenta:

- In a small saucepan, warm the milk and water together. In a non-stick saucepan, add the oil and polenta - stir fry for 4 minutes. Carefully add the warm milk and water mixture, a little at a time, mix well and keep stirring until the mixture is smooth.
- Lower the heat, cover the saucepan and cook for a further 4 minutes – add the salt and cheese.
- Remove to a greased, shallow non-stick baking tray, spread it evenly to a thickness of 15mm, and leave the mixture to cool.

For the mushroom stir-fry:

- In a non-stick saucepan - or a wok, add olive oil, butter, caraway seeds and the sliced mushrooms. Stir-fry on high heat for a few minutes until the mushrooms are cooked. Season well and add the chopped parsley or basil. If you have some tomato sauce, add 4 tablespoons of this to the mushrooms and mix well.

To serve:

Smear a little olive oil on the polenta, cut into two slices. Sauté the polenta slices on a griddle pan till golden, or brown under a hot grill.

Serve the mushrooms on the polenta and garnish with grated cheese.

* Polenta can be cooked early and left in the fridge – sauté just before serving.

Saffron Rice

Plain boiled rice can be transformed into the most fragrant, eye-catching dish in minutes. Serve it with a natural yogurt or Tomato and Avocado Raita (page 48).

Rice is a slow release carbohydrate that maintains a healthy blood sugar level for a long time.

Serves 4 - 6

225g Basmati rice	2-3 bay leaves
1 teaspoon saffron strands	2-3 cinnamon sticks
2-3 tablespoons oil	3 cardamon pods - split open
50g cashew or pistachio nuts	1 teaspoon cumin seeds
1 large onion - thinly sliced	1 tablespoon frozen peas
2 dry red chillies	½ teaspoon salt

- Wash the rice and soak in cold water for 10 minutes, drain well before cooking. Soak the saffron strands in 1 tablespoon warm water.

- Cook the rice uncovered in a large pan of boiling water for 10 minutes, until just tender. Strain the rice well and spread out on a large tray to cool (about 10 minutes). Rice is too sticky to stir-fry when it has just been cooked, so it is best to let it get cold first.

- Meanwhile, heat the oil in a wok or a deep frying pan, and stir-fry the nuts for 2-3 minutes until golden. Remove with a slotted spoon and set aside.

- Add the onion to the same pan and fry until crisp and golden. Drain on kitchen paper and set aside.

- Add a little more oil to the pan if necessary and stir-fry the chillies, bay leaves, cinnamon sticks, cardamon pods and cumin seeds. Then add the peas, cooked rice and the soaked saffron with its liquid and salt. Stir well to coat all the grains thoroughly and heat through.

- Transfer to a large serving dish and garnish with the onion and cashew or pistachio nuts.

Baked Sweetcorn with Asparagus

Sweetcorn is a unique grain, it contains zinc and **five important carotenoids** – alpha carotene, beta carotene, beta-cryptoxanthin, lutein and zeaxanthin. With such powerful phytonutrients, I hope you get into the habit of eating sweetcorn regularly. The simplest and easiest way is to serve fresh sweetcorn on the cob with a seasoned butter – yum, yum, yum!

Asparagus is a natural diuretic, it helps prevent water retention, plus it contains folate, vitamin C and potassium.

I have been cooking this baked dish for years - it is now re-enforced with the knowledge that it is so full of goodness.

Serves 2 - 4

For the white sauce:
2 tablespoons olive oil
2 tablespoons plain flour
425ml whole or semi-skimmed milk
1 teaspoon French mustard
salt to taste
freshly ground black pepper

280g corn niblets – fresh or tinned
12 small asparagus spears
half a red pepper – finely sliced
100g mature cheddar cheese - grated
2 small baking dishes or 1 big baking dish – 26cms by 16cms approximately

- Pre-heat the oven to 200°C, 400°F, Gas Mark 6.

- To prepare the white sauce warm 2 tablespoons of olive oil in a non-stick saucepan and add the plain flour. Cook for 3 minutes, then add the milk, and simmer for 10-12 minutes until the sauce thickens. Use a non-stick whisk to mix it well. Add in the French mustard and season with salt to taste and plenty of freshly ground black pepper.

- Mix the corn niblets (if using fresh corn, steam the corn niblets before mixing) with the white sauce and add half the grated cheese.

- Pour the mixture into a baking dish. Cover with the remaining cheese and garnish with the asparagus and the sliced red peppers.

- Bake, uncovered for half an hour or less, until the cheese bubbles.

* If large asparagus are available, trim the asparagus tips into 8cm lengths for garnish. Cut the rest of the asparagus spears into bite size pieces and mix in with the corn and white sauce mixture.

Baked Sweetcorn with Asparagus

Spiced Oats

Oats are an excellent source of complex carbohydrate that provides a continuous flow of energy. The soluble fibre in oats helps to stabilise blood sugar by slowing the amount and pace of sugar entering the blood stream, which is beneficial for those with type 2 diabetes. It also protects against heart disease by helping to lower cholesterol levels.

The usual way to take oats is in porridge in the morning but this recipe of spicing it gives it a savoury flavour. Spiced oats is a quick dish to cook and this filling dish can be served for a Sunday brunch - it will be difficult to guess that it is porridge oats.

Serves 2 - 4

80g porridge oats	salt to taste
2 tablespoons oil	½ teaspoon chilli powder
1 small red onion	1 teaspoon garam masala
1 teaspoon ginger	½ teaspoon lime juice

- Mix 80g oats (1 cup) and 400ml (2 cups) water in a saucepan. Bring it to the boil and simmer the porridge for 5 minutes, stirring occasionally.

- Finely chop the red onion and grate the ginger.

- In a wok, warm 2 tablespoons oil and sauté the onion till brown. Add the ginger and the cooked porridge – mix well.

- Add the salt, chilli powder, garam masala and lime juice to taste.

- Serve it hot.

  * Another recipe using oats is Nut & Dry Fruit Flapjacks (page 128).

Naan Bread

Ready-made naan is easily available now from supermarkets, but there is nothing like a fresh, hot, home-made naan covered with melting butter, nuts and coriander. This recipe is simplicity itself and my students are amazed at how easy it is to make their own naan bread.

Makes 10 Naan

225g self-raising or wholemeal flour
1x7g sachet easy-blend dried yeast
½ teaspoon salt
3 tablespoons natural yogurt
1 tablespoon oil

3-4 tablespoons warm water
a little butter (optional)
a few flaked roasted almonds or fresh
coriander leaves (optional)

- In a glass bowl, mix the flour, yeast, salt, yogurt and oil with enough warm water to make a soft dough. Cover and let it rest in a warm place for 25 minutes. The risen dough can be left in the fridge until you are ready to roll the naan breads. Extra dough freezes well.

- When you are ready to make the naan, knead the dough for 2 minutes until it is smooth. Then take a small ball of dough, the size of a golf ball, and roll it out to the shape of a small pitta bread. Repeat until you have about 10 naan.

- Cook them under a hot grill for about 2 minutes on each side, until they puff up like balloons. Alternatively dry roast the naan in a non-stick frying pan on both sides.

- Brush the naan with a little butter, garnish with almonds and coriander leaves if you wish, and serve. (Use garlic butter if available).

* Top Tip for raising the dough: A good tip I use in my class to keep the dough in a warm place is to heat up an oven for 10 minutes, switch it off completely. After 5 minutes, place the dough in a glass bowl, cover it and put it in the warm oven for 25 minutes. The dough will double in size.

Chapter 9

Introduction	124
Almond and Celery Soup	126
Tahini Dip	127
Nut, Seed and Dry Fruit Flapjacks	128
Baklava	129
Cinnamon Spiced Nut Bread	130
Apple, Fig, Walnut and Honey Parcels	132
Date and Nut Roll	133
Masala Roasted Nuts and Pumpkin Seeds	134
Peanut, Potato and Coriander Stir-fry	135

Nuts
& Seeds

Selection of Nuts and Seeds

Introduction

People are surprised when I suggest that a selection of nuts and seeds should be included as part of a daily vegetarian diet. Even though nuts are high in calories, the nutritional health benefits put them in the star food category. Nuts and seeds are a good source of protein and fibre, and contain the powerful antioxidant **vitamin E**, and **EFA omega 3** and **omega 6**. These essential fatty acids, omega 3 and omega 6, which the body cannot make have anti-inflammatory properties and play an important role in the prevention of cardio vascular diseases.

Try to eat a handful of nuts at least 5 times a week, sprinkle them on salads or pasta dishes or use them as suggested in my recipes. Enjoy raw nuts or roast nuts, on a moderate heat only, for high temperatures can destroy the omega 3 content.

I always keep a combination of almonds, pumpkin seeds, sunflower seeds, sesame seeds and organic linseeds in a jar – handy to munch when peckish.

Below is a list highlighting the goodness of popular nuts and seeds:

NUTS
Almonds one of the best nut sources of vitamin E which has powerful anti-inflammatory properties; they are a good source of protein, fibre, iron, potassium and magnesium. Almonds are known for their anti-ageing properties so, to keep the glow on the skin and body, remember to eat almonds regularly if not most days. They also help to increase memory.

Brazil nuts are rich in selenium, a powerful antioxidant, which helps to reduce heart disease. Eating 2-3 brazil nuts every day provides the RDA of selenium, which activates an antioxidant enzyme called glutathione perioxidase this may help to protect against cancer. Selenium also regulates the thyroid hormone and protects against clogging of the arteries.

Cashew nuts are high in iron, a mineral which is essential for the blood.

Hazelnuts are a rich source of vitamin E, an antioxidant, and contain monounsaturated fat which is similar to olive oil and helps to prevent heart attacks. They also contain fibre which is essential for a good digestive system and vitamin B (biotin) which is good for healthy skin and hair. Hazelnuts also contain a good quantity of manganese and zinc which are involved in another antioxidant enzyme called superoxide dismutase, which helps to delay atherosclerosis.

Macadamia nuts are rich in manganese and also contain monounsaturated fat which has been shown to reduce the risk of strokes and high blood pressure.

Peanuts are legumes (pulses) but they have a similar nutritional value to nuts, therefore, I have included peanuts in this chapter. Peanuts contain protein, vitamin E, fibre, calcium, copper, iron, magnesium, folate and zinc.

Peanuts are good for diabetics because the fibre and magnesium help to balance insulin and glucose levels.

Pistachio nuts are high in fibre, zinc (essential to boost the immune system), B vitamins, iron, potassium, co-enzyme Co-Q10 and vitamin E. Co-enzyme Co-Q10 acts as an antioxidant and helps all cells to use oxygen more efficiently. It is most important for people who have angina and for people who have already had a heart attack.

Pecan nuts contain zinc and vitamin E which help to protect against heart attack.

Walnuts have the highest antioxidant activity compared to all the other nuts. They are a rich source of plant derived omega 3 (alpha linolenic acid) which helps to thin the blood and prevents clots from forming (it works in a similar way to aspirin). Omega 3 is also anti-inflammatory.

SEEDS

Linseeds (Flax seeds) are a rich source of plant derived omega 3 and omega 6 fatty acids. Omega 3 is a natural blood thinner, it helps to protect the heart and protect against inflammatory diseases like arthritis. Linseeds contain lignans which helps to prevent hormone related breast cancer. Sprinkle one or two tablespoons of grounded linseeds on yogurt and try to eat it every day – it is a great way for vegetarians to obtain omega 3 and omega 6 essential fatty acids.

Pumpkin seeds are an excellent source of iron and zinc which strengthen the immune system; help to protect against prostate cancer; and contain the essential fatty acid omega 3 and omega 6 which promote a healthy heart. Make sure the man in your life eats pumpkin seeds regularly for it may provide protection from prostate cancer.

Sunflower seeds are rich in protein, vitamin E (25g contains 95% of RDA of vitamin E), B vitamins, iron, zinc, potassium, selenium and omega 3 essential fatty acid.

Sesame seeds contain high levels of iron and calcium which protect against osteoporosis, and they also contain vitamin B3 and omega 3 essential fatty acid. Black sesame seeds have anti-inflammatory properties.

Research shows that people who eat nuts and seeds regularly are less at risk of developing heart diseases, diabetes, cancer and other chronic ailments. I have selected a few unusual recipes using nuts and seeds, and hope you enjoy eating them in moderation, raw as well as cooked.

Inflammation is a critical factor in cardio vascular disease for it causes the complication of atherosclerosis. The anti-inflammatory activity of omega 3 and omega 6 essential fatty acids may play an important role in the prevention of cardio vascular disease.

Almond and Celery Soup

I love the crunch of fresh celery sticks but it takes forever to eat, so I created this tasty soup which I have been cooking for years. The soup is a great way of getting the nutrients of the celery - celery contains a lot of fibre and is the best diuretic vegetable, helping to reduce water retention. Almond is the best source of vitamin E and the addition of almonds gives this soup a creamy texture and a superb nutty flavour.

Serves 4

I tablespoon olive oil	300ml milk
I bunch celery	600ml vegetable stock or water
I big potato	salt to taste
30 whole almonds – skinned	freshly ground black or white pepper

- Clean the celery stalks and peel off some of the fibrous parts of the celery, especially on the outer celery sticks. Save some of the leafy tops for garnish. Chop the celery and potato into small pieces.

- In a large saucepan, add I tablespoon of olive oil and the vegetables. Sauté gently for 4 minutes. Add the skinned whole almonds, and continue to cook for a further 4 minutes, stirring frequently.

- Add 300ml milk and 600ml water and cook for 20 minutes until the vegetables are soft. (Do not cover the pan as the milk mixture might overflow).

- Season with salt and pepper to taste. Use an electric hand-blender or a liquidiser to purée the soup.

- Serve hot with leafy celery tops as a garnish.

Almonds

Tahini Dip

Tahini is available in most supermarkets and is used as a dip with falafel or pitta bread. Tahini is made from sesame seeds, which are full of iron, calcium, vitamin B, folate and omega 3.

To make a healthy, tasty dip, mix 4-6 tablespoons of tahini with iced cold water plus a little flat leaf parsley, and blend it until it's a runny, thin tahini dip. Store it in a jar.

Tahini can also be used as a dressing with mixed salad leaves or serve it with mixed roasted vegetables (like aubergines, courgettes, red onion and coloured peppers).

* For tahini dressing use equal quantities of tahini and natural yogurt, a little olive oil, lime juice, water, salt and freshly ground black pepper.

Nut, Seed and Dry Fruit Flapjacks

Flapjacks are a treat to eat, easy and economical to make at home and have the goodness of oats, nuts and seeds. Each little flapjack is packed with nutrients and handy to carry around for a quick dose of energy.

Makes 24 Small Flapjacks

Baking tin – 26cm by 16cm
(or bigger size tin for thin flapjacks)
150g butter
50g soft brown sugar
100g approx. golden syrup
250g porridge oats
50g desicated coconut

50g walnuts – chopped
50g macadamia nuts
50g dried apricots – chopped
25g dry cranberries
20g pumpkin seeds
20g sesame seeds
20g sunflower seeds

- Pre-heat the oven to 200°C, 400°F, Gas Mark 6.

- In a saucepan, melt the butter, sugar and syrup over a low heat until it is well mixed. Add the oats, all the nuts, seeds, dry fruits and berries. Mix thoroughly until well combined. (Use any combination of nuts, dry fruits and seeds that you prefer as long as the proportion of ingredients is the same – 150g of nuts, 75g of dry fruits and 60g of seeds).

- Spoon the mixture into the greased baking tin and press firmly.

- Bake for 20 minutes for a soft flapjack, and 25-30 minutes for a crispy flapjack - allow to cool.

- Cut into small squares or any shape you prefer. Store in a tin.

* For extra health benefits, spread melted good quality chocolate (above 70% cocoa) on top before cutting.

Chocolate is high on ORAC score, which is a measure of a food's antioxidant value. Chocolate is not only gorgeous but full of flavonoids and can help prevent heart problems.

Baklava

This mouth-watering honey-drenched pastry is very sweet and best served with a strong cup of coffee. For the filling, chopped walnuts can be used instead of almonds and pistachio nuts.

Serves 8

Non-stick baking dish – approx size
  26cm by 16cm
1 packet filo pastry
50g chopped almonds
50g chopped pistachio nuts
1 tablespoon butter
2 tablespoon caster sugar
1 teaspoon ground cinnamon powder
3 tablespoon butter or less, melted

For the syrup:
75g sugar
1-2 tablespoons honey
1 tablespoon lime juice
2 cinnamon sticks
1 cup water

- Pre-heat the oven to 200°C, 400°F, Gas Mark 6.
- Finely chop the almonds and pistachio nuts in a blender to bread crumb consistency.
- Warm 1 tablespoon butter in a saucepan and add the chopped almonds, pistachio nuts, caster sugar and cinnamon powder, cook for 4 minutes.
- Melt 3 tablespoons of butter in a small pan, use this to brush on each filo pastry.
- Unroll the filo pastry and cover well to prevent it from drying out. Take 4 sheets, cut to the size of the baking dish and brush each sheet of pastry with melted butter and layer them in a baking dish.
- Sprinkle half the above nut mixture on top. Take another 4 sheets of pastry and repeat.
- Cover it with the remaining mixture. Finally top with another 4 sheets of buttered pastry. Press down firmly.
- Using a sharp knife, score the top layer of the pastry into diamond shapes. Bake for 20-25 minutes until golden on top. Remove from the oven.
- In the meantime, prepare the syrup by mixing together the sugar, honey, 1 cup water, the cinnamon sticks and the lime juice in a saucepan. Boil rapidly until it forms a thin syrup - approx 10 minutes.
- Allow the syrup to cool. Pour the syrup over the pastry. Cut through all the layers using a sharp knife and serve. Alternatively serve 1-2 teaspoons of the syrup on each baklava pastry when ready to eat. This way the baklava stays very crisp.

Cinnamon Spiced Nut Bread

If you have never baked bread, follow this recipe and you will be smiling, for the result is a stunning show piece. Your friends will find it hard to believe it's home-made. Once tasted all your friends will ask for the recipe, it's a bread you cannot stop eating! It keeps in the fridge for 3-4 days, This wonderful bread is ideal with my spicy Butternut Soup (page 71), or eat it toasted and buttered with a hot cup of tea. This recipe makes approximately a 30cm loaf.

3 cups of strong white bread flour
plus 1 tablespoon extra flour for coating the raisins and cranberries
3 sachets of 1x7g each, easy-blend dried yeast
¾ cup warm milk
75g sugar
pinch of salt
2 tablespoons raisins

1 tablespoon red dry cranberries
5 full tablespoons mixed nuts - eg.
pistachio nuts, cashew nuts, macadamia nuts and walnuts – cut into bite sized pieces
1 teaspoon cinnamon powder
Baking dish 38cm by 28cm

- Soak the raisins and cranberries in cold water for 15 minutes, drain the water, pat dry and cover with 1 tablespoon of flour.

- In a glass bowl, mix 3 cups of flour, yeast, warm milk, sugar and salt, either by hand or use an electric blender, (add extra warm water if needed) to prepare a soft smooth dough. Cover the dough with a clean tea towel or grease proof paper and set aside in a warm place until double in size, approximately 30 minutes.

- Add the flour coated raisins, cranberries, mixed nuts and cinnamon powder to the dough, knead it and shape into an oval loaf. Place it on a baking dish, cover the dough, and let it rise again for 30 minutes.

- Pre-heat the oven to 200°C, 400°F, Gas Mark 6.

- Bake uncovered for 20-25 minutes until lightly brown. To check if the bread is cooked, lift it out of the baking dish, tap it a little on the bottom of the loaf and it should sound hollow.
Allow to cool before cutting into very thin slices.

Cinnamon Spiced Nut Bread

Apple, Fig, Walnut and Honey Parcels

This is an exotic, quick and very easy dessert, using filo pastry - use chilled filo pastry if available.

Makes 6

50g butter
1-2 dessert apples – skinned and cubed
3 dry figs – chopped
1 tablespoon chopped walnuts
1-2 tablespoons honey

1 teaspoon cinnamon powder
1 tablespoon sugar
12 filo pastry squares - each 10cm x 10cm
icing sugar for dusting

- Pre-heat the oven to 200°C, 400°F, Gas Mark 6.

- In a saucepan melt 25g of butter and add the apples, figs, walnuts, sugar, honey and cinnamon powder– let it all cook until soft, approx 10 minutes, then allow to cool.

- Melt 25g butter in a small pan for use on the filo pastry.

- Lay 2 squares of filo pastry on top of each other, brushing each sheet with a little melted butter. Spoon some apple mixture into the centre of the pastry, draw up the edges to form a parcel. Brush with a little melted butter. Repeat to make the rest of the parcels,

- Place on a baking dish and bake for 10-12 minutes, until golden on top.

- Dust with icing sugar.

- Serve with vanilla ice-cream or cream.

Walnuts

Date and Nut Roll

This sweet needs no sugar or butter, the natural sweetness of the dates is enough. The addition of mixed nuts turns it into a very nutritious and healthy snack. The recipe was created by my mum's younger sister, my aunt Manju Masi, a great influence in my life and a well known cook who always inspires me. It is extremely easy to prepare, needs hardly any cooking except for mixing all the ingredients and shaping it into a Swiss roll. Cut and eat it at your leisure, ideal for carrying in a bag when travelling.

Makes 2 Rolls

250g packet of seedless dates

250g mixed nuts – almonds, pistachio nuts and cashew nuts

8 tablespoon single cream

6 rich tea biscuits

2 big pieces of aluminium foil (for rolling and shaping)

- Roast the mixed nuts in a moderately hot oven for 8-10 minutes, then cool the nuts. Chop into bite size pieces, for example approximately three pieces from each almond.

- Chop 4 of the biscuits by hand, into bite sized pieces.

- Crush 2 of the biscuits in a blender or use a rolling pin, until bread crumb consistency - this will be used to cover the outside of the date and nut roll.

- Break the seedless dates into small pieces by hand, making sure there are no stones.

- In a big saucepan, mix in the date pieces and 8 tablespoons of cream, warm gently until it becomes a soft consistency (approximately 10 minutes).

- Add the mixed chopped nuts and the biscuit pieces, mix well and switch off.

- When the mixture is cold enough to handle, shape it like a thin Swiss roll. This amount makes 2 Swiss rolls each approximately 25cms in length.

- Spread some biscuit crumbs on the aluminium foil. Roll one of the date and nut rolls in these crumbs and use the foil to cover the roll, pack it tightly and keep in the fridge until ready to eat. Repeat the procedure for the second roll.

- Cut into thin rounds approximately 1cm thick and serve.

- It is a very handy sweet that keeps in the fridge for up to 4 weeks.

Masala Roasted Nuts and Pumpkin Seeds

Use any combination of nuts, for example, almonds, cashew nuts, peanuts and pumpkin seeds.

This masala (mixture of spices) nuts and seeds can be stored in a jar for one week, if not tempted to eat the whole lot in one go!

> 200g of mixed nuts
>
> 50g pumpkin seeds
>
> 2 tablespoons vegetable oil
>
> spices:
>
> salt to taste
>
> ½ teaspoon red chilli powder
>
> 1 teaspoon freshly ground pepper
>
> 1 teaspoon cumin powder
>
> 1 teaspoon coriander powder
>
> 1 teaspoon amchoor powder (dry green mango powder) - optional

- Pre-heat the oven to 200°C, 400°F, Gas Mark 6.

- Dry-roast the nuts and seeds separately for 5-10 minutes until brown.

- In a small saucepan, add oil, mix in the nuts and seeds until all are covered with a little oil. Add all the above spices to taste, and mix everything well.

- Let the nuts and seeds cool, and then serve.

Peanut, Potato and Coriander Stir-fry

Peanuts are good for people who have type 2 diabetes. Use raw, whole peanuts with the red skin on as they have a lot more fibre content and gives an extra colour to the dish. If raw peanuts are not available, use salted peanuts but remember not to add salt to the cooked dish.

The combination of dry coriander seeds and fresh coriander leaves in this quick stir-fry gives it an instant oriental flavour and a concentrated taste of coriander.

Serves 2

8 small potatoes
1 tablespoon oil
1 teaspoon coriander seeds, crushed
50g peanut kernels
2 tablespoons fresh coriander leaves
salt to taste
½ teaspoon red chilli powder
1 teaspoon lime juice

- Boil or steam the potatoes, drain and cut into small cubes.

- In a wok, warm the oil over a medium heat. Stir in the coriander seeds and peanuts, and cook until brown, for about 5 minutes. Add the potatoes, fresh coriander leaves, salt to taste, chilli powder and stir-fry for 5 minutes.

- Season with lime juice and serve warm with a side salad.

Glossary

Rainbow Fruits and Vegetables

To obtain a wide range of phytochemicals, it is recommended to eat a **"rainbow of colours"** every day - that is one fruit and/or vegetable from each of the 7 rainbow colours.

Here are a few suggestions of the fruits and vegetables – think of all the bright colours and the antioxidant properties.

Red:
Beetroot, cherry, cranberry, pink grapefruit, pomegranate, radish, raspberry, red grape, red cabbage, red kidney bean, red onion, red pepper, rhubarb, strawberry, tomato and watermelon.

Orange:
Apricot, carrot, cantaloupe melon, orange, paw-paw, pumpkin, squash and sweet potato.

Yellow:
Banana, corn, mango, pineapple, the spice turmeric and yellow pepper.

Green:
Apple, asparagus, avocado, broccoli, cabbage, celery, cucumber, fennel, grape, green pepper, kale, kiwi fruit, lettuce and spinach.

Blue:
Blueberry.

Indigo and Violet:
Aubergine, blackberry, blackcurrant and prune.

Eating a varied and balanced diet is the key to preventing numerous chronic diseases and keeping in optimum health.

Vitamins

Vitamins - a Latin word meaning "Life giving amines". Vitamins are organic substances consisting of essential micronutrients. Most are obtained from the food we eat but some can be produced within the body, for example vitamin D is produced when skin is exposed to sunlight. Vitamins are divided into 2 groups; the fat/oil soluble and the water soluble vitamins.

The fat/oil soluble vitamin A, vitamin D, vitamin E and vitamin K can be stored in the body.

The water soluble vitamin B group (B1, B2, B3, B6, B12, folate (folic acid), pantothenic acid, biotin) and vitamin C dissolve in water. These vitamins are not stored by the body, (except B12) the excess is excreted in urine so they need to be replenished daily.

RDA (Recommended Daily Allowance) is a rough guide to the minimum amount of vitamin and minerals required to prevent nutritional deficiencies in healthy adults.

Pre-biotic and Pro-biotic

Soup is the best lunch dish especially in cold weather. So many vegetables can be used to cook interesting and tasty soups. Some of my favourite soups are included in the book. The base of the soup is usually prepared with onions, leeks, garlic and tomatoes which are all rich in **pre-biotics** – these are plant sugars known as oligosaccharides. These plant sugars are not digested by the stomach acid but help to build up the growth of healthy, good bacteria **(pro-biotics)** in the gut which help our digestion. These "good" bacteria help to keep the balance between themselves and the billions of harmful bacteria that also live in the gut. The disruption of this delicate balance can lead to various illnesses. Pro-biotics "good" bacteria support the body's defences and improve the immune system. Eat yogurts that contain live bacteria that have pro-biotic properties.

Other foods rich in pre-biotics include asparagus, chicorys, bananas, cucumbers, chickpeas, sunflower seeds, whole wheat and milk, which stimulate the growth of lactic acid bacteria.

Spices

The usual spices used in Indian cooking are **black mustard seeds, cumin seeds, asafoetida, fenugreek seeds, ajwain seeds, turmeric, red chilli powder, dhana jeera** (a combination of two-parts of coriander powder to one-part of cumin powder) and **garam masala** (the simplest garam masala is made by dry roasting equal amounts of cumin seeds, cinnamon sticks, black pepper corns and slightly less cloves. Grind the mixture in a coffee grinder, sieve and store in an airtight bottle).

I was brought up in an Indian household with delicious tasty food cooked by my elder sister, Lalitaben, my younger sister, Shaila, and my brother Dhiroobhai's wife, Shashi. I always assumed that spices were just there for colour and flavour, to excite the palate. Now, through my research into the nutritional side of spices, I am amazed by the super nutrients in each one of the spices. For example, if my mum had asked me to take a quarter teaspoon of turmeric everyday, I would not have been able to obey her and would tend to forget it, but unknowingly, in cooking Indian food it is a part of my normal diet. Research work suggests that turmeric is antibacterial, antiviral, antiparasitic and is now known as anti-cancerous. It is one of the most important medicinal spices.

I believe that the colourful and tasty Indian cuisine, which has developed over thousands of years, was created so that unknowingly, one eats the herbs and spices and benefits from their range of antioxidants. These antioxidants neutralise different kinds of free radicals, therefore it is better to take a variety of spices to help protect against the development of chronic diseases.

Spices such as cinnamon, cloves and bay leaves (all used to make garam masala), may help to control blood sugar, so theses spices are excellent for anyone with **diabetes.**

Chilli peppers contain the chemical capsaicin which can help to **reduce cholesterol** and **triglycerides.**

Some **spices,** for example, cloves, garlic, ginger, thyme, oregano and rosemary, **protect against heart attack** by reducing the stickiness of platelets and help to thin the blood. The antioxidants in spices, especially spices like turmeric, ginger and black pepper, also have **anti-inflammatory properties,** which help to reduce inflammation and also help the body to get rid of toxins that can trigger inflammation. Turmeric contains compounds called **curcuminoids,** which help reduce inflammation and boost the powerful antioxidant glutathione to neutralise free radicals.

Spices like cloves, cinnamon, oregano and thyme for example have a varying degree of **antimicrobial activity** in their essential oils and by eating a variety of these spices one can guard against a range of bacterial and viral pathogens.

Certain spices such as common black pepper, are **strong bioavailability enhancers,** helping to absorb other important components from other spices – in this way one can increase the range of protective chemicals in the diet and boost the body's ability to use them.

Latest research has found that **salicylic acid,** the active ingredient in aspirin, **occurs**

naturally in Indian food which is cooked with spices. I hope I have convinced you and excited your taste buds to start eating curries as often as possible to get the super nutrients from the spices - it may help to spice up your life as well!

Selection of Spices

Cholesterol, Fats and Oils

Cholesterol is a yellow fatty substance, mainly produced by the liver, it is important for the production of hormones, helps to synthesise vitamin D and is needed for the proper functioning of every cell in the body. Most of the cholesterol in the body is carried by two proteins called Low Density Lipoprotein (LDL or bad cholesterol) and High Density Lipoprotein (HDL or good cholesterol). Good cholesterol helps to carry cholesterol away from the tissue to the liver, which is then excreted from the body. Bad cholesterol goes the other way, from the liver to the cells, where it can get oxidised and produce free radicals. Research work suggests that the **oxidation process** results in the cholesterol being deposited in the walls of the blood vessels, causing them to fur up and that can eventually lead to cardio vascular diseases. If the cholesterol level rises, the LDL bad cholesterol also rises, and there are more chances of it being oxidised. Evidence has shown that an unhealthy balance between the HDL and LDL cholesterol can lead to heart disease.

Diet can play a major role in the regulation of cholesterol levels. Latest research suggests that in order to lower cholesterol one should try to reduce the intake of saturated fat which stimulates the liver to produce cholesterol. Also a specific combination of proven cholesterol reducing foods when consumed regularly can have a great effect on cholesterol levels, similar to cholesterol lowering medicines prescribed by doctors. This includes **soluble fibre** from foods such as oats, bean based soups, houmous and vegetables like okra, aubergine and avocado, which all help to bind the cholesterol in the digestive tract and remove it from the body. **Plant sterols** found in most fruits and vegetables, are similar to the structure of cholesterol and help to reduce the absorption of cholesterol from the intestine – but they should be consumed regularly for the benefits to continue. Also one ounce of **nuts,** especially almonds, which are rich in the "cholesterol lowering" mono-unsaturated fat, plant sterols and fibre, if consumed regularly help to reduce cholesterol. The **antioxidant vitamin E** in the nuts also helps to reduce the oxidation of LDL cholesterol.

One can reduce the risk of having a heart attack by maintaining normal blood levels of cholesterol, triglycerides and homocysteine. Raised levels of homocysteine are found in people who are deficient in folate, vitamin B6 and vitamin B12. Folate is found in all green vegetables and beans; B6 is found in avocados, bananas, carrots, lentils, soya beans, wheatgerm and sunflower seeds; and for vegetarians the best source of B12 is cheese and organic milk. To stay healthy, check your cholesterol, triglyceride and homocysteine levels regularly with your doctor.

Fats & Oils

The edible fats and oils in our diet contain a combination of different fats, saturated, monounsaturated and polyunsaturated fat and are made up of chemicals called triacylglyceroles. These are made up of smaller molecules known as fatty acids, which consist of a chain of carbon atoms, with some hydrogen and oxygen atoms attached at various places. Fats are a ready store of energy. Fats form important components of our body tissue and provide the basis for the manufacture of many important chemicals and hormones. Without fat one cannot absorb the fat soluble vitamins A, D, E and K from food.

Fat is the most concentrated form of energy available to humans – it contains 9 calories per gram (protein and carbohydrates contain 4 calories per gram). Expert opinion suggests not to consume more than 70g of fat for an active woman and 95g for a man, daily. To avoid obesity, coronary heart disease and various forms of cancer, one should monitor the amounts and the kinds of fats one eats.

Saturated fat is the type most connected with heart problems (mainly from animal sources - butter) and is usually solid at room temperature. Coconut and palm oil contain medium chain saturated fatty acids and are now known as "starfoods". Research suggests that these fats are digested quickly and not stored in the body.

Unsaturated fats, especially monounsaturated fats with one bond are considered much healthier (the less bond in a fatty chain, the less chance of it being oxidised by free radicals). Unsaturated fats are liquid at room temperature.

Monounsaturated fats with one double bond in its carbon chain, is found in olives, avocados and most nuts; it helps to lower bad LDL cholesterol and raises the good HDL cholesterol.

The **polyunsaturated fatty acids,** with 2 or more double bonds in their carbon chain are usually plant oils eg groundnut oil, sunflower oil, corn oil etc. and have also been shown to lower bad LDL cholesterol.

Two important polyunsaturated essential fatty acids are **omega 3** (alpha linolenic acid) and **omega 6** (also known as linoleic acid). They cannot be made in the body and must be included in the diet. They help every cell in the body to function and are vital for the growth and development of the brain and nervous system. Numerous studies show that omega 3, found in oily fish, linseeds and walnuts helps to lower total cholesterol, bad LDL cholesterol and triglycerides. It is a natural blood thinner and also inhibits platelet derived growth factors that form plaque and block the arteries.

Transfats are hydrogenated vegetable oils that have been treated to give the characteristics of saturated fat and are solid at room temperature. They are mainly found in processed foods like biscuits and are thought to increase the risk of heart diseases, in a similar way to saturated fats. Transfats should be avoided where possible.

It is recommended to use olive oil and groundnut oil for cooking and for vegetarians to eat nuts and linseeds to obtain the essential fatty acids, omega 3 and omega 6.

Recipe suggestions

Soups

Almond and celery soup 126

Barley and red lentil broth 113

Butternut squash, ginger and cinnamon soup 71

Chickpea and yogurt soup with guacamole 99

Kale soup with broccoli 27

Roasted tomato and red pepper soup 45

Tuscan white bean soup with rosemary 100

Salads

Bulgar wheat salad with coriander, parsley, mint and walnuts 115

Buckwheat, hazelnut and three bean salad 103

Good food salad 30

Pea, mint, feta cheese salad with roasted butternut squash, red peppers, pumpkin seeds and quinoa 104

Pesto pasta salad 31

Puy lentils with herb chutney 101

Red cabbage coleslaw 22

Spiced sprouting bean salad 102

Spinach, fennel, orange and roasted nut salad with oriental dressing 35

Stir-fry chinese cabbage and kohlrabi with walnut dressing 23

Chutney – dips

Houmous 107

Cabbage, carrot and mango relish 21

Spicy tomato salsa 43

Tomato and avocado raita 48

Tahini dip 127

Starters

Carrot, beetroot, apple and turmeric juice 67

Cinnamon spiced nut bread 130

Cocktails

    fresh mango juice with ginger 89

    apple and cranberry spritzer 89

    watermelon granita 89

    mango lassi 89

Falafel 108

Masala roasted nuts and pumpkin seeds 134

Oven baked sweet potato chips 73

Spicy fenugreek and coriander fritters 33

Spinach and feta parcels 37

Soya bean pods – edamame 62

Tomato and garlic bruschetta 47

Light meals for lunch or side dishes

Aubergine caponata 80

Baked sweetcorn with asparagus 119

Broad beans, baby asparagus and green beans in mint sauce 77

Cabbage and couscous parcels with carrot sauce 19

Chinese style ginger pak choi 32

Green bean, mangetout, baby corn and pine nut stir-fry 78

Indian pancakes with cabbage, carrot and mango relish 20

Moroccan style green lentils 109

Naan bread 121

Peanut, potato and coriander stir-fry 135

Spiced oats 120

Stir-fry quinoa with peppers 76

Stuffed mushrooms with a medley of coloured peppers 74

Tomato baked with herb pesto 51

Tomato, onion and
potato gratin with oregano 52

Main courses and side dishes

Black-eye bean curry 105

Broccoli and potato curry 15

Cabbage and celeriac curry 16

Cauliflower and cashew nut curry 17

Chilli tofu 61

Globe artichoke with mushroom 82

Green risotto with courgette
and tomato salsa 39

Golden tofu with coconut curry sauce 58

Okra and mixed peppers jalfrezie 79

Penne arrabiata 49

Polenta and mushroom stir-fry 116

Roasted tofu with
spring onion and cashew nuts 57

Saffron rice 117

Spicy soya bean curry 59

Stir-fried spinach curry 36

Stuffed mediterranean vegetables 84

Tomato and green pepper curry 53

Desserts

Apple, fig, walnut and honey parcels 132

Avocado fool with pistachio nuts 92

Baklava 129

Carrot halwa 85

Carrot pumpkin halwa 85

Cinnamon poached pears 91

Date and nut roll 133

Dry fruit compote 90

Nut, seed and dry fruit flapjacks 128

Pomegranate with yogurt shrikand 95

Bibliography

Wiley Encyclopaedia of Food Science & Technology 2000 – 2nd Edition. Edited by Federick J Francis; ISBN 0471 – 19285 – 6; Vol 1-4.

Cancer & Nutrition. Kini Prasad, WC Cole; ISBN 9051993773 (1OS Press); Van Diemenstraat 94, 1013 CN Amsterdam Netherlands.

Lampe, JW (1999) Health effects of vegetables & fruit: assessing mechanisms of action in human experimental studies. *Am J Clin Nutr.* 70(3), 475S-490S.

Halvorsen BL et al (2002) A systematic screening of total antioxidants in dietary plants. *J Nutr.* 132(3), 461-71.

Liu H (2004) Potential synergy of phytochemicals in cancer prevention: mechanism of action. *J Nutr.* 134 (12) 3479S-3485S.

Talalay P, Fahey JW (2001) Phytochemicals from cruciferous plants protect against cancer by modulating carcinogens metabolism. *J Nutr.* 11 30275-335.

Temple NI Antioxidants & disease:more questions than answers. *Nutr Res.* (2000), 20:449-459.

Joshipura KJ et al (2001) The effects of fruit & vegetables intake on risk for coronary heart disease. *Ann. Intern Med.* 134(12); 1106-14.

Jessica K Campbell etc (2004) Tomato phytochemicals & prostate cancer risk. *J Nutr.* 134(12)3486S-3491S.

Greenworld Peter (2004) Clinical trials in cancer prevention current results & perspectives for the future. *J Nutr.* 134(12)3507S-3511S.

Jean Carper, Food your Miracle Medicine, London, Simon & Schuster, 1994 First Edition.

Lisa Turner, Meals that Heal, Healy Nuts Press, 1996, Vermont, ISBN 089281-6252.

Paul Schulick, Ginger Common Spice & Wonder Drug, 3rd Edition, Holm Press, ISBN 1-890772-07-0.

Spiced Sprouting
Bean Salad